PUB GRUB

PiE

George Darbyshire

PUB GRUB

COSY AND COMFORTING RECIPES TO MAKE AT HOME

EBURY PRESS

Contents

Hi! I'm George, a self-taught cook from Buxton, Derbyshire, a little town up in the hills where the weather's rarely on your side. It's home to our family fish and chip shop, The Coach House – first bought by my nan over fifty years ago and later taken on by my parents – and that's really where my love for food started. I literally grew up surrounded by the smell of pie, chips and gravy. I learned early on that good food is about flavour, comfort and the people you share it with – the laughter, the noise and those moments around a table when everything else fades away.

I never planned to do this for a living. I worked a lot of jobs, went travelling, ate my way around half the world, and somehow found myself back in my kitchen filming recipe videos on my own with just my phone. I taught myself to cook properly by watching and reading, and I learned mostly by getting it wrong a few times first. Let's just say if you post something on the internet and you've messed it up, people are more than happy to point it out.

What started as a few foodie photos posted on social media turned into something much bigger: a community of people who share a passion for proper, comforting food. That same love of bringing people together also led my best mate Jake and me to start Eat in the Park, a food and music festival in Buxton that began as a mad idea during lockdown and grew into something that brought thousands together every summer. It showed me how powerful food can be, how it brings people together, creates memories and connects communities.

Pub Grub is my first cookbook – even writing that sentence feels surreal. The idea came from the food I've always loved, the kind you'll find in a proper British pub. Hearty, comforting and full of flavour, with a few simple twists of my own. These are the dishes that will bring everyone around the table: Sunday roasts, casual Friday-night suppers, family dinners or meals for those quiet evenings when you just need something that hits the spot.

Every dish in here tells a bit of my story, from growing up in the chippy, to living in Italy, to the recipes I've discovered travelling and the twists I've made my own back at home. It's the kind of food that brings people together and puts smiles on people's faces, that will fill your kitchen with life and the sort of delicious aromas that make a house a home – or at least make your neighbours jealous.

This book is for everyone who loves pub food, whether you're cooking for the family, your mates, or just yourself after a long day. It's honest, hearty and a little rough around the edges, the way good pub grub should be.

So grab a drink, put the oven on and let's get cooking!

George

Here's What's Going On

This book brings together everything I love about British pub food: good, hearty comfort dishes – the classics. But as well as all the old favourites, I've mixed in some new ideas and a few twists along the way, so you'll find northern staples like slow-cooked Steak & Kidney Suet Pudding as well as quick ideas like Sausage & Cheese Toast, when you just want something simple but satisfying. Some recipes take time and care, others come together in minutes, but they've all got one thing in common – they're full of flavour. There are a few that I could not live without: the Treacle Sponge with Stem Ginger & Citrus Zest is pure nostalgia – light, sticky and sweet; the Chicken, Leek & Bacon Pie is everything you want from classic home cooking; and my Tartare Sauce, which I could honestly eat with a spoon.

Here's how the book is laid out:

LIGHT BITES
Starters, snacks and small plates – from sausage rolls and savoury scones to Scotch eggs and bar snacks that pair perfectly with a pint.

THE CLASSICS
The dishes every pub menu should have. Think bangers and mash, toad in the hole and fish and chips done properly.

THINGS ON TOAST
Because not everything has to be fancy. Simple ingredients piled on to good bread can make some of the best meals going.

PROPER PIES
Shortcrust, suet, puff – you'll find them all here. With deep fillings, golden pastry and plenty of gravy, a proper pie is the ultimate comfort food.

ONE-POT WARMERS
Stews, casseroles and slow-cooked dishes for those nights when you want something rich and comforting.

THE SPECIALS BOARD
A few recipes that go beyond the classics – the kind of dishes you might find scrawled on the chalkboard at your favourite local.

NOT JUST ANY POTATOES
Mash, chips, roasties, dauphinoise – this section's all about celebrating the humble spud and the many ways to make it brilliant.

ANY SIDES WITH THAT?
All the extras that bring a dish together – condiments, sauces and seasonal veg done right.

PERFECT PUDDINGS
From crumbles to custards, steamed puddings and tarts, this is where the comfort factor goes up another level.

Cook's Notes

I've tried to keep the recipes as clear and consistent as possible so you can cook them just as I do at home. Here are a few notes to keep things simple:

Ingredients

Unless stated otherwise. . .

- Eggs are large and free-range.
- Butter is unsalted.
- Parsley is flat-leaf parsley.
- Milk is whole milk.
- Cream is double cream.
- Bacon is smoked streaky bacon.
- Flour is plain flour, unless the recipe calls for self-raising.
- Potatoes are Maris Piper variety.
- Herbs and spices are dried.
- Sugar is granulated or caster (where appropriate). If a specific type is needed (golden, muscovado, demerara), it'll be specified.
- Garlic cloves are medium size.
- Onions are brown onions.
- Stock means good-quality shop-bought stock or stock cubes made to packet instructions.
- Olive oil for dressing and finishing should be good-quality extra virgin olive oil; use regular olive oil for cooking.
- I use flaky salt in my cooking. If you're using table salt, go steady – it's stronger and you'll need less.
- When zesting citrus fruits, use unwaxed fruit where possible.

Tips and techniques

- Always read a recipe before starting – some steps can be done ahead or overlapped to save time.
- Always taste as you go and season with salt and black pepper – I don't over-salt recipes, so adjust as needed to your liking.
- When frying, use vegetable or sunflower oil, not olive oil.
- For deep-frying, the oil temperature is essential – if you don't have a thermometer, drop a small cube of bread into the hot oil: at roughly 180°C it should turn golden in about 30 seconds.
- Fresh herbs should be roughly chopped rather than minced to a paste – I like to see flecks of herb in my food.
- Grated cheese means coarsely grated, unless finely grated is specified (for example, for a sauce).
- When a recipe says 'chill in the fridge', it means uncovered unless otherwise stated (for example, with pastry or meat).

Essential Equipment

I like having a well-stocked kitchen. You don't need everything on this list, but these are the bits I reach for most often when cooking the recipes in this book. Some are everyday essentials; others are worth investing in if you cook a lot – they'll make life easier and help you get better results.

Weighing scales
Digital thermometer (for meat, frying oil and sugar)
Wooden spoon
Silicone spatula
Whisk
Tongs
Ladle
Peeler
Kitchen scissors
Box grater
Microplane or fine grater (for citrus zest, nutmeg and cheese)
Rolling pin
Sieve
Colander
Mixing bowls (a few sizes)
Chopping boards (ideally one for meat and one for veg)
Good, sharp knives (a chef's knife and a small paring knife will cover most things)
Skewer (for testing cakes and puddings)
Jug for measuring liquids
Roasting tray (a large, deep one and a smaller one)
Baking trays (at least two flat ones)
Ovenproof dishes (medium and large for things like shepherd's pie and lasagne)
Casserole dish (for stews, pies and slow braises)
Frying pans (one large non-stick, one smaller)
Pans (small, medium and large – lids are useful)
Stockpot (for soups and boiling joints)
Loaf tin (900g/2lb)
Cake tins (20cm and 24cm will cover most things)
Tart tin (24cm and 28cm loose-bottomed)
Muffin or Yorkshire pudding tin
Pie dish (ceramic or metal)
Baking beans or dried rice (for blind baking pastry)
Wire cooling rack
Baking paper, cling film and foil
Food processor or stick blender
Hand mixer or stand mixer (beneficial but not essential)
Pastry cutters (a glass works fine too)
Kitchen timer (or your phone)

The Bits I Always Have In

Every cook has their own set of staple ingredients, the things that live in the cupboard, fridge or drawer and quietly find their way into almost everything they make. They tell you a lot about how someone cooks. Mine is a mix of the British stuff I grew up with and a few bits I've picked up over the years from travelling and researching recipes. These are the ingredients that make up the backbone of most dishes in this book.

Mustard – English, Dijon, Wholegrain and Powdered
English mustard gives you that fiery kick that pairs perfectly with a slice of roast beef. Dijon is smoother, great whisked into a dressing or stirred through a creamy sauce. Wholegrain adds warmth and texture; I use it loads with pork or in honey-mustard glazes. And English mustard powder is always worth having around, it's great for mixing into rubs, sauces or mash when you want that sharp heat without the extra liquid.

Vinegar – Malt, Red Wine and Cider
Malt vinegar basically runs in my blood and is a must for chips. Red wine vinegar is brilliant in dressings and sauces, and cider vinegar brings a bit of tang to chutneys and marinades. Each has its own personality, and they all add balance to heavier flavours.

Stock or Stock Cubes – Beef, Chicken and Vegetable
You can't beat the depth a good stock adds. I keep all three types to hand: beef for rich sauces and gravies, chicken for soups or pies, and vegetable for a lighter touch. Homemade or fresh stock is great if you have it but gel pots, cubes or powder are fine – they're quick, consistent, and save a lot of time.

Worcestershire Sauce
There's barely a week that goes by that I don't use it. Tangy, savoury and slightly sweet, it adds a hit of umami to pies, gravies, marinades and sauces. A dash in a stew or a splash on cheese on toast – it just works.

Wine – Red and White
A splash of wine can transform a sauce or gravy. Red wine adds depth and richness to beef or lamb dishes, while white wine brings brightness and acidity to creamy sauces, as well as to chicken and fish. It doesn't need to be fancy, just something you'd happily drink. And if there's a bit left in the bottle afterwards, well . . . it'd be rude not to.

Flour – Plain and Self-Raising
Plain flour for roux, batters and sauces; self-raising flour when baking cakes, scones or puddings. If you've got both, you're sorted for pretty much anything.

Cornflour
Perfect for thickening sauces, gravies or pie fillings. Mix it with a bit of cold water first before adding it to hot liquid, so it doesn't clump.

Sugar – White, Light and Dark Brown, Caster and Icing
I use a range of sugars depending on what I'm making. White sugar for balancing savoury sauces or adding sweetness to marinades; light and dark brown for a deeper, toffee-like flavour in puddings, crumbles and glazes; caster sugar for baking sponges and meringues; and icing sugar for dusting or finishing desserts. Each one brings its own character and texture, and they all earn their place in the cupboard.

Oils – Olive and Vegetable
Olive oil for salads, marinades and finishing dishes; vegetable oil for frying and roasting. They each bring something different in terms of flavour and cooking style, so it's worth keeping both around.

Condiments – Ketchup, Brown Sauce, Mayonnaise and Hot Sauce
These have all earned their place in the British fridge for good reason. Ketchup, brown sauce and mayo often find their way into sauces and marinades, but they're just as good on the side if that's your preference. And a splash of hot sauce never goes amiss when something needs a bit of a kick.

Salt and Pepper
I use flaky salt for most of my cooking – it seasons evenly and gives a clean, sharp finish. If you're using table salt instead, just go steady as it's much finer and can overpower a dish quickly. Freshly cracked black pepper adds warmth and bite, while white pepper works well in lighter sauces where you don't want the specks showing.

Butter
Always unsalted so you can control the seasoning. Butter adds richness and body to everything from mash to pastry. It's essential – and yes, I go through a lot of it.

Dried Herbs and Spices
Flavour is everything, and the right mix of herbs and spices can make a dish sing. I try to use fresh where I can, but dried is often more convenient – especially for slow-cooked dishes and sauces. I often use dried thyme and sage, smoked paprika for depth and colour, cumin for warmth, and a touch of nutmeg for creamy sauces or puddings. Garam masala, curry powder, turmeric and chilli powder also have a place – they add gentle heat and aroma that lift a dish without overpowering it. Simple, versatile, and all you really need.

Nuts
I always keep a few bags of nuts in the cupboard – they're great for adding texture, flavour and a bit of richness when you need it. Walnuts and flaked almonds work well in salads, crumbles and stuffings, while hazelnuts are brilliant with chocolate or roasted veg. A handful toasted in a dry pan can completely change a dish, whether it's sweet or savoury.

A Few Extras I Can't Be Without
Jarred horseradish and Marmite for adding depth to gravies and sauces, mango chutney or a good traditional chutney for sandwiches or to serve alongside something rich, and a bag of sultanas for bringing a touch of sweetness to desserts or savoury dishes.

Chapter One

LIGHT BITES

Runny Yolk Scotch Egg with Mustard Whisky Cream

SERVES 4

PREP 40 mins

COOK 20 mins

Easily my favourite pub snack. If I see a Scotch egg on the menu, in any form or flavour, that's usually me sold. There's nothing quite like breaking through the crisp, golden shell to find a soft, runny yolk inside. This one keeps it classic but adds a rich mustard and whisky cream on the side that brings a bit of warmth and sharpness – perfect with a pint.

---

4 eggs
6 quality pork sausages
15g fresh parsley, finely chopped
10g fresh sage, finely chopped
1½ tbsp Dijon mustard
1 tsp salt
1 tsp black pepper
50g plain flour
2 eggs, beaten
100g panko breadcrumbs
2–3 litres vegetable oil, for frying

For the mustard whisky cream:
1 tbsp olive oil
½ shallot, finely chopped
1 shot single-malt whisky
Juice of ½ lemon
1 tbsp honey
1½ tbsp wholegrain mustard
1 tsp English mustard
1 tsp white wine vinegar
½ tsp black pepper
½ tsp salt
3–4 tbsp mayonnaise

● **Time-saving tip:** *Cook and chill the eggs in advance; they peel more easily and make assembly quicker.*

Bring a pan of water to the boil and lower in the eggs. Cook for 5 minutes if you want the yolks runny, or 6 if you prefer them a little firmer. Transfer straight into a bowl of iced water to stop them from cooking, then peel carefully once cool.

Squeeze the sausage meat from the skins into a bowl. Mix with the parsley, sage, Dijon mustard, salt and pepper until evenly combined. Divide into 4 portions and flatten each into a disc large enough to wrap around an egg. Place an egg in the middle of each disc and mould the meat evenly around it, making sure there are no gaps. Chill for 30 minutes to firm up.

Set up three shallow bowls, one with the flour, one with the beaten eggs and one with the panko. Roll each chilled Scotch egg first in flour, then egg, then breadcrumbs. Press gently so the coating sticks, then chill again while you heat the oil.

Half-fill a deep pan with oil and heat to 160°C. Fry the eggs in batches for 6–8 minutes until crisp and golden brown all over. Drain on kitchen paper.

To make the mustard whisky cream, heat the olive oil in a small pan and add the shallot. Cook until soft, then pour in the whisky and carefully flambé with a lighter. Once the flames die down, add the lemon juice, honey, both mustards, vinegar, pepper and salt. Stir to combine, then take off the heat and mix in the mayonnaise until smooth.

Slice the Scotch eggs in half and serve with the mustard whisky cream spooned or drizzled alongside.

Beef & Pork Sausage Roll with Sweet Smoky Ketchup

MAKES
4

PREP
30
mins

COOK
55
mins

This is my take on the classic sausage roll, with beef, pork, sharp Cheddar and mustard all wrapped in golden pastry. The filling's rich and full of flavour and the sweet smoky ketchup on the side takes it up another notch. They're versatile too, perfect warm from the oven on their own, dipped into the ketchup, packed up for a picnic or paired with a cold pint. However you have them, these sausage rolls are a step above.

400g beef mince
400g sausage meat
100g mature Cheddar, grated
1 beef stock cube, crumbled
1 small onion, grated
1 tbsp Worcestershire sauce
1 tsp English mustard
1 sheet of ready-rolled puff pastry
1 egg yolk, for brushing
1 tsp fennel seeds
1 tsp sesame seeds

For the ketchup:
1 small garlic bulb
Olive oil
2 tbsp tomato purée
200g passata
1 tbsp red wine vinegar
1 tbsp soft light brown sugar
1 tbsp Worcestershire sauce
1 tsp smoked paprika
½ tsp chilli powder
Salt and black pepper

● **Cost-saving tip:** *Skip the Cheddar or halve the meat quantity and bulk out with fine breadcrumbs if making a bigger batch.*

Start with the ketchup. Preheat the oven to 200°C/180°C fan. Cut the top off the garlic bulb, drizzle with olive oil and season with salt and pepper. Wrap it in foil and roast for 40–45 minutes until soft and golden. Let it cool.

Heat a touch of oil in a pan, add the tomato purée and cook for a minute before adding the passata, vinegar, sugar, Worcestershire sauce, smoked paprika, chilli powder and some salt and pepper. Simmer for 10–15 minutes, then squeeze in the roasted garlic and blend until smooth with a stick blender. Set aside.

For the sausage rolls, mix the beef mince, sausage meat, grated Cheddar, crumbled stock cube, grated onion, Worcestershire sauce and English mustard in a bowl until well combined.

Unroll the puff pastry and cut it in half across the shorter side so that you've got two rough squares. Lay a line of the meat mixture along one side of each, dividing it evenly between the squares. Brush the opposite edges with egg yolk, fold the pastry over and seal, making sure the seams are underneath. Cut each roll in half so you've got four chunky sausage rolls (or cut in quarters for 8 smaller ones like in the photo opposite). Place on a sheet of baking paper, brush the tops with more egg yolk and sprinkle with the fennel and sesame seeds.

Turn the oven up to 210°C/190°C fan. Transfer the sausage rolls (keeping them on the baking paper) to a shallow baking tray and bake for 25 minutes, then remove the paper and continue cooking for an additional 10 minutes until the bases are crisp, the pastry is golden and the sausage rolls are cooked through.

Serve with a generous spoonful of the smoky ketchup.

Fishcakes with Poached Egg & Lemon Chive Butter

SERVES
4

PREP
40
mins

COOK
30
mins

These take me back to when my wife Rosie and I first got together. We'd travel back and forth 100+ miles midweek from Buxton to Lichfield to see each other, and dinner was usually something simple: supermarket fishcakes with a poached egg, a bottle of white wine and the two of us chatting at the table. No fancy butter sauce back then, but it always felt like a treat. This version keeps the heart of it with a few elevated touches.

400g skinless cod fillets
300ml whole milk
2 bay leaves
2 garlic cloves, crushed
½ lemon, sliced
400g Maris Piper potatoes, peeled and chopped
2 spring onions, finely chopped
2 tbsp capers, roughly chopped
1 tbsp chopped dill
1 tbsp chopped parsley
2 tbsp mayonnaise
80g mature Cheddar, grated
Plain flour, for dusting
2 eggs, beaten
100g dried breadcrumbs
Vegetable oil, for frying
Salt and black pepper

To serve:
4 eggs, for poaching
2 large handfuls of pea shoots

For the lemon chive butter:
100g butter
Juice of ½ lemon
1 tbsp Dijon mustard
1 tbsp chopped chives

Place the cod in a shallow pan with the milk, bay leaves, garlic and lemon slices. Simmer gently for 8–10 minutes until the fish is just cooked through. Lift it out with a slotted spoon and place it on kitchen paper to drain and cool completely.

Boil the potatoes in salted water for about 15 minutes until soft, then drain and leave them in the colander to steam dry. Once fully dry, lightly mash them – just enough to break them down.

In a mixing bowl, combine the flaked cod, cooled mash, spring onions, capers, dill, parsley, mayonnaise and some salt and pepper. Chill the mixture for 15 minutes if you can – it helps firm it all up. Shape into 4 large patties, pushing a quarter of the grated Cheddar into the centre of each one and sealing it in. Dust each patty in flour, dip into the beaten egg, then coat in breadcrumbs.

Preheat the oven to 200°C/180°C fan. Fry the fishcakes in a pan with a little oil over a medium heat until golden on both sides, then transfer to the oven for 10 minutes to warm through and melt the cheese. While they're in the oven, poach your eggs.

To make the lemon chive butter, melt the butter in a small pan until just bubbling, then take off the heat. Add the lemon juice and Dijon mustard and whisk to emulsify into a smooth sauce. Stir through the chopped chives.

Serve the fishcakes on pea shoots, topped with a poached egg and a spoonful of the warm lemon chive butter.

- **Cost-saving tip:** *Any firm white fish will do the job – try pollock, coley or frozen basa fillets for a cheaper fish that still flakes.*

Stilton Scones with Fig Chutney

MAKES
4–6

PREP
30
mins

COOK
20
mins
(+ 50 mins for chutney)

I've always been more of a savoury person, so here I've given the classic scone a bit of a twist. Crumbly Stilton gives the dough loads of flavour, and when these scones are warm out of the oven with a spoonful of fig chutney, it just works. We may not be able to agree on how to pronounce scones, but we should be able to agree on how good these taste!

275g self-raising flour, plus extra for dusting
1 tsp baking powder
½ tsp salt
1 tsp mustard powder
50g cold butter, cubed
120g Stilton, crumbled (80g for the dough, 40g for topping)
1 egg
120ml whole milk, plus extra for brushing
Black pepper
Cream cheese, to serve

For the fig chutney:
250g fresh figs, chopped
50g dried figs, chopped
1 eating apple, peeled and finely diced
½ onion, finely diced
80g light brown sugar
120ml cider vinegar
Pinch of salt

Start with the chutney. Add all the ingredients to a pan and bring to a gentle simmer, then cook over a low heat, uncovered, for about 50 minutes, stirring occasionally, until thickened and sticky. Remove from the heat and use a stick blender to pulse the mixture just enough to break it down while keeping some texture. Set aside to cool.

Preheat the oven to 220°C/200°C fan and line a baking tray with baking paper. In a mixing bowl, combine the flour, baking powder, salt, mustard powder and a good crack of black pepper. Rub in the butter with your fingers until the mixture looks like coarse breadcrumbs. Stir through 80g of the crumbled Stilton.

In a jug, whisk the egg with the milk, then pour into the dry mix. Bring it together gently using a butter knife – just enough to form a soft dough without overworking it.

Turn the dough out on to a floured surface and pat it to about 3cm thick. Cut out 4–6 rounds using a cutter, reshaping the dough as needed. Transfer to the tray, brush the tops with a little milk and scatter over the remaining 40g of Stilton.

Bake for 15–18 minutes until golden and risen. Serve warm, split open with a generous layer of cream cheese and a spoonful of fig chutney. Perfect for a snack, a picnic, or as part of a cheese board spread.

● **Cost-saving tip:** *If you haven't got Stilton, use whatever cheese you've got knocking about in the fridge – just steer clear of anything too soft or with a high moisture content, or the scones won't hold their shape.*

Stout-Battered Mushy Pea Fritters with Mint Jelly Vinegar

SERVES
4

PREP
40
mins
(+ overnight soaking)

COOK
20
mins

My dad does all sorts of fritters at the chippy, but these are one of the most popular. This is my take on them – creamy, old-school mushy peas made from scratch, battered in a rich stout mix and fried until crisp. The mint jelly vinegar on the side is sharp, sweet and nostalgic; it cuts through the richness perfectly and ties the whole thing together. Great as a starter or as a snack with a pint.

For the mushy peas:
120g dried marrowfat peas
1½ tsp bicarbonate of soda
½ tsp salt
½ tsp sugar

For the batter:
150g plain flour, plus extra for dusting
1 tsp baking powder
1 tsp salt
200ml stout
Vegetable oil, for deep-frying

For the mint jelly vinegar:
3 gelatine leaves
200g sugar
240ml malt vinegar
20g mint leaves, very finely chopped
1 tsp salt
½ tsp white pepper

- **Time-saving tip:** *You can use tinned mushy peas instead of making them from scratch. They won't have quite the same depth of flavour, but you'll still end up with a cracking little starter.*

Start with the peas. Soak them overnight in cold water with 1 teaspoon of the bicarbonate of soda.

While the peas are soaking, make the mint jelly vinegar so it has time to cool and set. Soak the gelatine leaves in cold water for 5 minutes. Meanwhile, combine the sugar and vinegar in a small pan and bring to a gentle simmer until the sugar dissolves, then remove from the heat. Squeeze out the excess water from the gelatine, then whisk it into the hot vinegar until fully melted. Stir in the chopped mint, salt and white pepper. Leave to cool and set to a firm, glossy jelly. You can pour it into small ramekins for individual portions or let it set in one dish ready to spoon on to the fritters.

The next day, drain and rinse the soaked peas well, then put them in a pan and cover with 1cm of fresh cold water. Add the remaining ½ teaspoon of bicarb, the salt and sugar, and simmer over a medium heat for about 30 minutes until soft and mushy. Leave them to cool completely so they firm up enough to shape. Once cool, shape the peas into small fritters or quenelles and chill in the fridge for 20 minutes so they hold their shape.

For the batter, whisk together the flour, baking powder and salt in a bowl. Slowly pour in the stout while whisking until the batter is smooth and thick enough to coat the back of a spoon.

Heat your oil in a deep pan or fryer to 180°C. Lightly dust the fritters in flour, dip them in the batter, and fry in batches for 3–4 minutes until golden and crisp. Drain on kitchen paper and season lightly with salt.

Serve the fritters hot, spooning the mint jelly vinegar over the top or alongside on the plate.

Roasted Beetroot & Goat's Cheese Salad

SERVES
4

PREP
15 mins

COOK
1 hour

Earthy, caramelised beetroot, sweet roasted onion, creamy goat's cheese and crunchy toasted walnuts, all tied together with a warm roasted garlic dressing. The textures are spot on and the balance of tangy, sweet and nutty makes it perfect for a quick midweek lunch or as a great starter when you've got people round.

600g beetroot
1 onion, halved
A few sprigs of fresh thyme
3 tbsp olive oil, plus extra for drizzling
2 tbsp red wine vinegar
1 garlic bulb, top sliced off
Salt and black pepper

For the dressing:
2 tbsp olive oil
1 tbsp red wine vinegar
1 tsp wholegrain mustard

To finish:
200g mixed salad leaves
120g goat's cheese, crumbled
80g toasted walnuts

Preheat the oven to 220°C/200°C fan. Wash the beetroot, but don't peel them. Place the whole beetroots into a roasting tray along with the halved onion and the thyme. Drizzle over the 3 tablespoons of olive oil and the vinegar, then season with salt and black pepper. Toss to coat and cover the tin tightly with foil. Roast for 1 hour.

At the same time, place the garlic bulb on a piece of foil, drizzle with olive oil, season with salt and pepper and wrap it up. Place it directly on an oven shelf and roast alongside the beetroot.

Once the beetroot is cool enough to handle, rub the skins off using kitchen paper – they should slide off easily. Cut the beetroot into wedges and slice the roasted onion.

To make the dressing, squeeze the roasted garlic into a jar and add the olive oil, red wine vinegar and mustard. Add a pinch of salt and pepper, seal with a lid and shake well.

Arrange the salad leaves on 4 plates and top with the beetroot wedges, sliced onion, goat's cheese and toasted walnuts. Drizzle over the dressing and serve.

Roasted Onion & Ale Soup with Cheese Bread Soldiers

SERVES
4

PREP
20
mins

COOK
1½
hours

My British take on French onion soup – rich with roasted onions, dark ale and beef stock – served with golden cheese soldiers for dunking. Perfect for a cold, wet day when you want to be sat by the fire, bowl in hand.

100g butter
1 tbsp olive oil, plus extra for brushing
6 large white onions, thinly sliced
2 garlic cloves, finely chopped
4 sprigs of fresh thyme
2 bay leaves
250ml ale
1.2 litres beef stock
1 tbsp Worcestershire sauce
1 tbsp cornflour mixed with 2 tbsp water
Salt and black pepper

For the cheese soldiers:
4 slices of thick-cut white bread
1 tbsp Dijon mustard (optional)
100g strong mature Cheddar, grated
100g Red Leicester, grated

Melt the butter with the tablespoon of olive oil in a large heavy-based pan over a medium heat. Add the onions with a good pinch of salt and cook them slowly, stirring now and then, until they're soft, deep golden and caramelised – this should take 45–60 minutes. Be patient here, this bit makes the soup.

Add the garlic, thyme and bay leaves and cook for another minute. Pour in the ale and let it bubble and reduce slightly, scraping the bottom of the pan to release all the flavour. Add the beef stock and Worcestershire sauce, then season with salt and pepper. Simmer gently for 30 minutes.

Stir in the cornflour mixture and let it cook for another 5 minutes to thicken. Remove the thyme and bay leaves and adjust the seasoning if needed.

For the cheese soldiers, preheat the grill and line a tray with foil. Lightly brush the bread slices with olive oil and toast one side under the grill until golden. Flip, spread with Dijon (if using) and pile on the cheeses. Grill until melted and bubbling, then slice into thick strips.

Ladle the hot soup into bowls and serve with the cheese soldiers stacked on the side – the ultimate dunk.

Mac & Cauliflower Cheese Bites with Bacon Crumb

MAKES
12

PREP
25 mins

COOK
35 mins

Mac and cheese is pure comfort, and cauliflower cheese is one of the best bits on a roast dinner, so wrapping them both up in golden breadcrumbs just felt right. The bacon crumb gives it that extra salty punch as well as texture. Great as a small plate, a starter, or piled up to share at a party, these are dangerously good.

250g macaroni
250g cauliflower florets
12 rashers of streaky bacon
90g butter
90g plain flour, plus extra for dusting
800ml whole milk
2 tsp English mustard
200g mature Cheddar, grated
150g mozzarella, grated
50g Parmesan, grated
2 eggs, beaten
150g breadcrumbs
Olive oil, for frying (optional)

Cook the macaroni in boiling salted water until just al dente, adding the cauliflower florets for the last 4 minutes of cooking, then drain.

Fry the bacon until crisp, then finely chop or crush half of it in a pestle and mortar for the crumb. Cut the rest into pieces and keep these to stir into the cheese sauce.

For the sauce, melt the butter in a pan, stir in the flour to make a roux, then gradually whisk in the milk until smooth and thick. Add the mustard, Cheddar, mozzarella and Parmesan, stirring until melted. Set aside a few ladlefuls of the sauce for topping later, then mix through the cooked pasta and cauliflower along with the reserved bacon pieces. Spread on to a tray to cool until firm enough to shape.

Shape into 12 equal-sized bites, roll them in flour, dip them in the beaten egg and coat them in the breadcrumbs. In a deep pan, heat the oil to 170°C and fry the bites in batches for 3–4 minutes, until deep golden and crisp. Lift out and drain briefly on kitchen paper.

Warm the reserved cheese sauce and spoon a little over each bite. Sprinkle with the bacon crumb and finish with extra cheese if you really want to go for it.

Carrot & Parsnip Bhajis with Sweet Curry Yoghurt

SERVES
4

PREP
20
mins

COOK
20
mins

Onion bhajis are one of my go-tos when I'm out for an Indian, but this little twist with carrot and parsnip gives you a touch of sweetness and a lighter, crispier finish. You still get that warmth from the spices, and the cooling curry yoghurt dip works brilliantly alongside them. Spot on as a snack or a starter to share with a cold beer.

200g carrots, grated
200g parsnips, grated
1 small onion, thinly sliced
2 garlic cloves, finely chopped
Thumb-sized piece fresh ginger, peeled and grated
150g plain flour
1 tsp baking powder
1 tsp ground cumin
1 tsp ground coriander
1 tsp ground turmeric
1 tsp chilli powder
150ml water
Vegetable oil, for frying
Salt and black pepper

For the curry yoghurt:
200g natural yoghurt
1 tbsp tikka curry paste
1 tbsp mango chutney
Juice of ½ lemon
Small handful of fresh coriander, chopped

Mix the grated carrot and parsnip with the onion, garlic and ginger in a bowl. Stir through the flour, baking powder and spices, then slowly add the water until you've got a thick batter that holds together. Season with salt and pepper.

Heat your vegetable oil in a deep pan to 160–170°C; if you drop in a small spoonful of your bhaji mix, it should sizzle gently and rise to the surface fairly quickly. If it sinks or turns brown instantly, adjust the heat. Using a spoon, carefully drop portions of the mixture into the oil and fry in batches until golden and crisp, about 4–5 minutes. Drain on kitchen paper.

For the dip, mix the yoghurt with the curry paste, mango chutney, lemon juice and coriander. Serve the bhajis hot with the yoghurt on the side.

Pork Belly Bites with Apple Cider Chutney

SERVES
4

PREP
15
mins
(+1 hour marinating)

COOK
55
mins

I've always had a thing for salty, fatty cuts of meat, especially pork when it goes crispy. Paired with sweet cider-spiked apple chutney, this is the kind of snack that hits every note: rich, sharp, sticky and moreish. These are made for sharing – piled high on a plate, passed round with a few ciders, and guaranteed to disappear fast.

1kg pork belly, skin removed, cut into bite-sized chunks
2 tbsp English mustard
1 tbsp Worcestershire sauce
1 tbsp olive oil
Salt and black pepper

For the apple cider chutney:
350g apples (about 2–3), peeled, cored and diced
½ onion, peeled and chopped
125g soft brown sugar or caster sugar
75g raisins
½ tsp mustard seeds
½ tsp ground ginger
¼ tsp chilli flakes
⅛ tsp salt
150ml cider vinegar

Rub the pork with the mustard, Worcestershire sauce, olive oil, a good grind of black pepper and a pinch of salt. Leave it to marinate in the fridge for at least an hour.

When ready to cook, preheat the oven to 200°C/180°C fan. Spread the pork belly pieces out on a wire rack set over a tray and roast for 50–55 minutes, flipping them halfway, until they are golden and crisp all over.

While that's in the oven, make the chutney. Combine the apples with all the other chutney ingredients in a large saucepan. Set over a medium heat and bring to the boil, stirring occasionally to dissolve the sugar.

Once bubbling, reduce to low, cover and simmer for 10–15 minutes until the apples have softened. Remove the lid and continue cooking for another 15–20 minutes, stirring often, until the liquid has mostly evaporated and the chutney is thick and glossy. If you like it smoother, pulse it briefly in a blender until it reaches the texture you want.

Serve the hot pork belly bites with a generous dollop of the apple chutney on the side.

● **Cost-saving tip:** *You can often get pork belly in large strips for less – just remove the skin yourself and cut it into chunks.*

Chapter Two

THE CLASSICS

Bangers & Mash

SERVES
2

PREP
15
mins

COOK
45
mins

A true British classic. Hearty sausages, creamy mash and rich onion gravy. The cider gives the sauce a gentle sweetness that balances the savoury sausages, while the mash ties it all together. As soon as the weather turns in autumn, this is one of those dishes that's on our menu at home until spring the following year. A class winter warmer and simple to do.

Olive oil, for frying
6 sausages
600g Maris Piper potatoes, peeled and cubed
100g butter
100ml milk

For the gravy:
6 tbsp butter, plus a knob to finish
3 onions, thinly sliced
500ml cider
250ml chicken stock (made with 2 stock cubes)
1 tbsp fresh thyme leaves
1 tsp Worcestershire sauce
Salt and black pepper

Preheat the oven to 200°C/180°C fan. Heat a little olive oil in a large ovenproof pan and fry the sausages over a medium heat for about 5 minutes until browned all over. Transfer them to a roasting tray and cook in the oven for about 10–12 minutes until cooked through.

Once the sausages are in the oven, prepare the potatoes, cover with cold salted water and bring to the boil. Simmer gently for about 20 minutes, or until tender.

While the potatoes cook, make the gravy. Melt the butter in the same pan in which you browned the sausages, add the onions and cook slowly for about 20 minutes until soft and golden. Pour in the cider and chicken stock, stir through the thyme and Worcestershire sauce and simmer for 15 minutes until thickened. Season with salt and pepper, then finish with a knob of butter.

When the potatoes are tender, drain and mash until smooth. Beat in the butter and milk with a wooden spoon until creamy, seasoning with a little more salt to taste.

To serve, pile the mash on to plates, top with the sausages and finish with plenty of the cider onion gravy.

Fish & Chips with Mushy Peas

SERVES
2

PREP
25
mins
(+ overnight soaking for peas)

COOK
55
mins

With my parents owning a chippy for over fifty years, I was brought up on fish and chips. So when it came to writing a cookbook, there was never any question about including this recipe. It's the dish that defines British food – crisp, golden fish in a light beer batter, proper chips, and a side of mushy peas. Simple, comforting and timeless, there's a reason it's a classic.

700g Maris Piper potatoes, peeled and cut into thick chips
Vegetable oil, for frying
150g plain flour, plus extra for dusting
30g cornflour
1 tsp baking powder
250ml cold beer
2 × 200g skinless pieces of cod fillet
Sea salt

For the mushy peas:
120g dried marrowfat peas
1 tsp bicarbonate of soda
¼ tsp salt
¼ tsp sugar

To serve:
Lemon wedges
Vinegar

Start by soaking the marrowfat peas overnight in cold water with ½ teaspoon of the bicarbonate of soda. The next day, drain and rinse, then tip them into a pan and cover with fresh water by a couple of centimetres. Add the remaining ½ teaspoon of bicarb, along with the salt and sugar. Simmer over a medium heat for 30 minutes until soft and mushy, then give them a gentle mash.

Soak the potato chips in cold water to wash off the starch. Bring a large pan of salted water to the boil and simmer the chips until just tender, about 20 minutes. Drain carefully and leave to steam dry on a rack, then chill in the fridge until needed.

Preheat the oven to 140°C/120°C fan and place a wire rack over a large baking tray. Heat your oil to 130°C in a deep pan, no more than halfway full. Fry the chips in batches for 5 minutes, until a light crust forms. Remove from the pan and drain them on a wire rack, then leave to cool. When ready to serve, turn the oil up to 180°C and fry the chips again for 5–7 minutes until golden and crisp. Spread the chips out on the wire rack, season with sea salt and transfer to the oven, but leave the door slightly ajar so that the steam escapes. They'll stay hot and crisp while you cook the fish.

Meanwhile, whisk the flour, cornflour, baking powder and ½ teaspoon salt together in a bowl. Gradually whisk in the cold beer until the batter is smooth. Heat the oil again to 180°C while you pat the cod dry, dust lightly in flour, then dip into the batter. Lower carefully into the oil and fry for 6–8 minutes until golden and crisp. Drain on a rack or kitchen paper.

Serve the fish with the hot chips, mushy peas and a wedge of lemon, plus salt and vinegar on the side.

Chip Shop Curry Sauce

SERVES
6

PREP
10
mins

COOK
35
mins

Not every chippy serves curry sauce. My parents' place actually does two – one fruity and chunky, the other a bit spicier and smoother. This version sits somewhere in between. It's warming, gently spiced and perfect poured over a steak pudding, a cheese and onion pie, or just all over chips with plenty of salt and vinegar. You really can't beat it.

Vegetable oil, for frying
1 large onion, finely diced
1 carrot, grated
4 garlic cloves, crushed
50g fresh ginger, peeled and grated
2 tbsp tomato purée
1 tbsp currants
1 tsp ground cumin
1 tsp ground coriander
1 tsp garam masala
1 tsp ground turmeric
½ tsp chilli powder
1 star anise
500ml chicken stock
200ml coconut milk
1 tbsp malt vinegar
1 tbsp soy sauce
1 tsp golden syrup
1 tbsp cornflour mixed with 2 tbsp cold water
Salt and pepper, to taste

Heat a splash of oil in a pan over a medium heat and fry the onion until soft and starting to turn golden. Add the grated carrot, garlic and ginger and cook for a few minutes until fragrant. Stir in the tomato purée, currants and all the ground spices and the star anise, letting them toast briefly to release their flavour.

Pour in the chicken stock, coconut milk, malt vinegar, soy sauce and golden syrup. Bring to a gentle simmer and cook for 20–25 minutes until everything has softened and the flavours have come together.

Remove the star anise, then use a stick blender to blitz the sauce to your preferred consistency. Some chip shop curries are smooth; others have a bit more texture – go with what you like best. Stir in the cornflour mixture and simmer for another couple of minutes until glossy and thickened. Season and adjust with a splash of water if needed to achieve the perfect chip shop-style base.

Scampi & Chips with Tartare Sauce

SERVES
2

PREP
30
mins

COOK
45
mins

This is one of those plates you'll find on nearly every chip shop and pub menu, and one I grew up on. This version is a bit more of a luxury, using fresh langoustines for the scampi. Crisp breadcrumbed tails, triple-cooked chips and a chunky tartare sauce to bring it all together.

---

3 large Maris Piper potatoes, peeled and cut into thick chips
750ml vegetable oil, for frying
30g plain flour
½ tsp garlic powder
½ tsp salt
12 langoustines, peeled and cleaned
1 egg, beaten
60g breadcrumbs
Sea salt

For the tartare sauce:
100g mayonnaise
10g tarragon, finely chopped
10g parsley, finely chopped
10g dill, finely chopped
15g pickled red onion (page 47), finely chopped
25g capers, roughly chopped
1 small gherkin, finely diced
Zest and juice of ½ lemon
2 tsp Dijon mustard
Salt and black pepper

Rinse the starch off the potatoes and boil in salted water until just tender. Drain, spread out on a tray and chill for 30 minutes. Heat the oil to 130°C and fry the chips for 5–6 minutes until a crust forms. Drain, cool, then fry again at 180°C until golden and crisp. Season with sea salt.

For the tartare, stir together all the ingredients. Season to taste and chill until ready to eat.

Mix the flour with the garlic powder and salt. Dust the langoustines in the seasoned flour, dip them in the beaten egg and coat them in the breadcrumbs. Heat the oil again to 180°C and fry the scampi in batches for 2–3 minutes until golden and crisp. Drain on kitchen paper.

Serve the scampi with a pile of triple-cooked chips and a generous dollop of tartare sauce.

● **Cost-saving tip:** *Using fresh langoustines makes this a proper luxury version. To bring the cost down, you can swap them for large prawns or chunks of firm white fish. The flavour and texture won't be quite the same, but it will still be tasty.*

Fish Finger Sandwich with Chunky Tartare Sauce & Rocket

SERVES
2

PREP
25
mins

COOK
25
mins

You never forget your first legal drink, and mine was in a pub in Manchester with a fish finger sandwich on the side – a simple pairing that always delivers. Here you're getting thick cod fingers fried until golden, a chunky tartare sauce piled high, a bit of rocket and a scattering of crispy shoestring fries for crunch.

---

1 litre vegetable oil
2 Maris Piper potatoes, peeled and cut into thin matchsticks
½ tsp sea salt
2 medium cod fillets, cut into 8 fingers
75g plain flour, seasoned with salt and pepper
2 eggs, beaten
100g panko breadcrumbs
Salt and black pepper

For the tartare sauce:
150g mayonnaise
15g tarragon, finely chopped
15g parsley, finely chopped
15g dill, finely chopped
25g pickled red onion (page 47), finely chopped
40g capers, roughly chopped
2 small gherkins, finely diced
Zest and juice of 1 lemon
1 tbsp Dijon mustard

To serve:
50g butter, softened
4 slices of crusty white bread
40g rocket
1 tbsp olive oil
½ tsp black pepper

Heat the oil in a deep pan to 180°C; if you drop a potato matchstick in and it sizzles gently (rather than sinks or instantly browns), you're good to go. Fry the potato matchsticks in batches for 3–4 minutes until crisp and golden. Drain on kitchen paper and sprinkle over the sea salt.

For the tartare, stir together all the ingredients. Season and chill until needed.

Dust the fish fingers in the seasoned flour, dip them in the beaten egg and coat them in the panko, pressing the panko on well. Heat the oil again to 180°C and fry the fish in a couple of batches for 4–6 minutes until golden and cooked through. Drain on kitchen paper.

Butter both sides of the bread slices and toast in a pan or under the grill until golden. Toss the rocket with the olive oil and black pepper.

To build the sandwich, spread chunky tartare on the toasted bread, add the rocket to the bottom slice, stack the fish fingers, sprinkle with shoestring fries and top with the other slice.

Corned Beef Hash with Fried Egg

SERVES
4

PREP
20
mins

COOK
35
mins

Corned beef hash has always been one of those proper comforting plates. Cheap, filling and warming, it is often thrown together from tins and leftovers. This version takes it up a notch with roast potatoes, giving a crunch that makes all the difference. The corned beef gets crisped up too, with mustard powder and Worcestershire sauce adding a punch of flavour. And of course it wouldn't be right without a fried egg on top and a little brown sauce on the side.

1kg floury potatoes, peeled and diced into 2cm cubes
3 tbsp olive oil
340g tin corned beef, cut into chunks
1 heaped tsp English mustard powder
50g butter
3 onions, thinly sliced
2 tbsp Worcestershire sauce
4 eggs
Salt and black pepper
Brown sauce, to serve

Preheat the oven to 220°C/200°C fan. Bring a pan of salted water to the boil and cook the potatoes for 8 minutes until just tender. Drain well and let them steam dry. Toss the potatoes in a bowl with 2 tablespoons of the olive oil and a touch of salt, then spread them out on a baking tray. Roast for 25 minutes until golden and crisp.

While the potatoes roast, toss the corned beef with the mustard powder. Heat the remaining tablespoon of olive oil in a large frying pan and fry the corned beef over a high heat for about 10 minutes until it is deeply crisp and browned. Lift it out and set it aside.

In the same pan, melt the butter. Add the onions and cook until softened and golden. Once the potatoes are ready, tip them into the pan with the onions, turn up the heat and season well with black pepper. Return the crispy corned beef to the pan, splash in the Worcestershire sauce and toss everything together. Let it fry a little longer so the flavours mingle.

Meanwhile, fry the eggs in a separate pan until the whites are set but the yolks are still runny.

Serve the hash topped with a fried egg and finish with a drizzle of brown sauce on the plate.

Beef Burger with Crispy Bacon, Mustard Mayo & Pickled Red Onions

SERVES
2

PREP
20
mins

COOK
15
mins

Burgers are a staple on most pub menus these days, and for good reason. This one's got smoky bacon, sharp mustard mayo and sweet pickled onions, all stacked in a soft toasted brioche bun. No cheese, no fuss. Just bold flavours and a proper satisfying bite.

500g beef mince (20% fat)
Salt and black pepper

For the pickled red onion:
100ml white vinegar
1 tsp salt
1 tsp sugar
6 black peppercorns
1 red onion, thinly sliced

For the mustard mayo:
3 tbsp mayonnaise
1 tsp English mustard
1 tsp wholegrain mustard
1 tbsp Worcestershire sauce
1 tsp Tabasco

To serve:
4 rashers streaky bacon
2 brioche buns
Butter, for toasting

Start by pickling the onion. Add the vinegar, salt, sugar and peppercorns to a small pan and bring to a simmer. Pour it over the sliced red onion in a bowl and leave to pickle.

To make the burgers, divide the mince into 4 equal portions and shape them into patties about 1.5cm thick. Press a slight dimple into the centre of each one with your thumb to help them cook evenly. Season well with salt and pepper.

Mix the mayonnaise, English mustard, wholegrain mustard, Worcestershire sauce and Tabasco in a bowl and set aside.

Get a pan or grill hot. Cook the patties for 3–4 minutes on each side until browned and cooked to your liking. At the same time, fry the bacon in a separate pan until crisp.

Slice the brioche buns in half and toast the cut sides in a pan with a bit of butter until golden.

To build, spread mustard mayo on the bottom half of each bun, add two patties per burger, top with crispy bacon and a tangle of drained pickled onions, then finish with the top bun.

- **Cost-saving tip:** *Buying mince and shaping your own patties at home works out cheaper than pre-made burgers, and it lets you control the fat content for optimal flavour and texture.*

Toad in the Hole

SERVES
1

PREP
15
mins

COOK
45
mins

A proudly British classic with a name that sounds like something out of a kids' book, but don't let that fool you. This is official pub grub. Crisp, golden batter puffed up around three good sausages, all soaked in a rich, smoky cider gravy that's nearly as much of a star as the main event. It technically serves one, but it's a generous portion, the sort of plateful that fills your belly and lifts your mood.

---

2 tbsp beef dripping
3 large sausages
75g plain flour
½ tsp salt
½ tsp white pepper
3 large eggs
165ml whole milk

For the gravy:
1 rasher of smoked streaky bacon, diced
Knob of butter, plus an extra knob to finish
½ red onion, thinly sliced
1 garlic clove, minced
1 sprig of thyme, leaves only
1 tsp Worcestershire sauce
250ml medium-dry cider
100ml beef stock
1 tsp wholegrain mustard

Preheat the oven to 240°C/220°C fan. Heat a small ovenproof frying pan over a medium heat and add 1 tablespoon of the beef dripping. Once hot, add the sausages and cook for 5–7 minutes, turning occasionally, until browned. Remove the sausages and tip the remaining beef dripping into the pan. Place it in the oven to get the fat smoking hot.

In a bowl, whisk together the flour, salt and white pepper. Crack in the eggs, then gradually add the milk while whisking until you have a smooth batter.

Carefully remove the hot pan from the oven, pour in the batter and arrange the sausages in the centre. Get it straight back into the oven and bake for 25–30 minutes until well risen and golden. Try not to open the door while it's cooking, or you'll lose the rise.

While that's in the oven, get your gravy going. In a pan over a medium heat, cook the diced bacon in the butter until the bacon starts to brown. Add the onion slices and cook for 5–10 minutes until softened. Add the garlic and cook for a minute, then add the thyme. Stir in the Worcestershire sauce, then pour in the cider and simmer until reduced by half. Add the stock and simmer for an additional 5 minutes, then finish by stirring in the mustard and butter until the sauce is glossy.

Cut into your golden Yorkshire and pour over plenty of that rich, smoky gravy.

Steak & Kidney Suet Pudding

SERVES 4

PREP 30 mins

COOK 3¾ hours

This is a classic northern chip shop dish, featuring soft suet pastry packed with beef, kidney and rich gravy. I'm sure some wouldn't have even heard of this dish (including my own wife); however, now it's her go-to from our chippy. In chippies, these puddings are typically served as smaller individual portions, but this is a giant one for four people, a real main event to bring to the table and cut open, letting the rich, luscious gravy ooze out.

---

2 tbsp vegetable oil
600g beef shin, diced
1 large onion, thinly sliced
200g lamb's kidney, trimmed and chopped
2½ tbsp plain flour
1 tbsp English mustard
1 tbsp Worcestershire sauce
350ml beef stock (made with 1 stock cube)
1 tbsp fresh thyme leaves
Salt and black pepper
Chips or mash and gravy, to serve

For the suet pastry:
250g self-raising flour
125g shredded suet
About 160ml cold water
Butter, for greasing

Heat the oven to 180°C/160°C fan. Warm the oil in an ovenproof casserole dish, brown the beef well, then add the sliced onion and cook until soft. Stir in the kidney, sprinkle over the flour, then add the mustard, Worcestershire sauce, stock and thyme leaves. Season with pepper, cover with a lid and place in the oven for about 1½ hour until the beef is tender. If the mixture looks a bit dry at this stage, stir in a splash of hot water, as a pudding should have plenty of gravy inside. Leave the filling to cool slightly.

Mix the flour, suet and a pinch of salt in a bowl, then gradually stir in the water until you have a soft dough. If it feels a bit dry, add an extra splash of water until it comes together easily. Grease a 1.5-litre pudding basin with butter. Roll out about two-thirds of the dough and use it to line the basin.

Spoon in the cooled meat mixture with its gravy. Roll out the remaining dough for the lid, place it on top and seal the edges. Run a knife around the edge of the basin to clean up and neaten the seal before covering with pleated baking paper and foil, tied tightly with string.

Set the basin in a large pan, add boiling water to come halfway up the sides, cover and steam gently for about 2 hours and 15 minutes, topping up with boiling water if needed. Remove carefully, unwrap and turn out on to a plate. Serve with chips or mash and plenty of gravy.

Beef Wellington with Red Wine Jus & Horseradish Cream

SERVES
4

PREP
45 mins
(+ cooling and chilling)

COOK
2 hours

This is a luxurious recipe that's a real showstopper, whether you've got guests coming round or a special meal on the cards. Rich beef wrapped with whisky-laced mushrooms, prosciutto and golden pastry is served with a glossy red wine jus and a punchy horseradish cream. It always feels a bit daunting slicing into one of these and hoping the beef is blushing pink in the middle, but when you get it right, there's no dish quite like it.

400g beef fillet
1 tbsp olive oil
2 tbsp Dijon mustard
25g butter
2 shallots, finely chopped
2 garlic cloves, finely chopped
250g chestnut mushrooms, finely chopped
50ml whisky
6 slices of prosciutto
350g puff pastry
Flour, for dusting
2 egg yolks, beaten
Salt and black pepper

Remove the beef from the fridge, pat it dry and season with salt and pepper. Heat a frying pan with the olive oil and sear the fillet all over until browned, about 2 minutes. Brush the beef with the Dijon mustard and leave to cool.

In the same pan, melt the butter and gently fry the shallots, garlic and mushrooms with a pinch of salt until all the liquid has cooked out. Pour in the whisky and let it bubble away, stirring until absorbed into the mushrooms. You want the mix thick and dry so it doesn't leak into the pastry. Leave to cool completely.

Lay out a sheet of cling film, then cover with slightly overlapping slices of prosciutto. Spread the mushroom mix evenly over the prosciutto, then place the beef in the middle. Using the cling film, roll it up tightly into a log. Chill for 30 minutes to allow the mixture to firm up.

Roll out the puff pastry on a floured surface into a rectangle large enough to wrap around the beef. Remove the cling film from the beef, place it on the pastry and wrap it up, tucking and pressing tightly to seal. Brush all over with beaten egg yolk, then score a pattern on the pastry with four evenly spaced lines lengthways and about six diagonals across to create a cross-hatch effect. Chill again for 15 minutes.

Preheat the oven to 200°C/180°C fan. Place the Wellington on a baking tray, brush once more with egg yolk and bake for 40 minutes. Leave to rest for 10 minutes before slicing.

For the horseradish cream:
1 fresh horseradish root, peeled and finely grated
200ml crème fraîche or sour cream (at room temperature)
1¼ tsp Dijon mustard
1 tsp cider vinegar
Pinch of caster sugar
1 tsp Maldon sea salt flakes or ½ tsp fine salt (or to taste)
25g chives, finely chopped

For the red wine jus:
2 tbsp olive oil
2 shallots, finely chopped
2 garlic cloves, finely chopped
2 sprigs of thyme
1 bay leaf
1 tsp tomato purée
300ml red wine
500ml beef stock
25g cold butter, diced

While the Wellington is in the oven, make the horseradish cream. Grate the horseradish root finely and stir it straight into the crème fraîche before it loses its punch. Mix in the Dijon mustard, cider vinegar, sugar and salt, then fold through the chives. Taste and adjust with extra horseradish or seasoning, depending on how fiery you like it. Cover and chill for 30 minutes before serving.

For the red wine jus, heat the olive oil in a pan over a medium heat and add the shallots and garlic. Cook slowly for about 5 minutes until softened but not coloured. Stir in the thyme, bay leaf and tomato purée, then pour in the red wine. Bring to the boil and let it reduce by two-thirds until slightly syrupy. Add the beef stock and simmer gently until the liquid has reduced by half and has a sauce-like consistency. Strain through a fine sieve into a clean pan, discarding the solids. Just before serving, whisk in the cold butter to give it a glossy finish, then season with salt and black pepper.

Slice the rested Wellington and serve it with the red wine jus poured over, accompanied by a spoonful of the horseradish cream on the side.

● **Time-saving tip:** *If fresh horseradish is tricky to find, a jar of shop-bought creamed horseradish will work. It won't have that fresh punch, but the star of the dish is the Wellington itself, so it's a fair shortcut when needed.*

Lamb Shanks & Mash with Mint & Port Gravy

SERVES
4

PREP
25 mins

COOK
3½ hours

There's something about slow-braised lamb shanks that makes them the ultimate winter warmer. The meat turns meltingly tender in the oven, the mash is smooth and buttery, and the gravy is rich with port and a hit of mint. It's got the feel of a Sunday roast, but with that pub-style comfort. Perfect for a cold evening, especially with a glass of Rioja.

---

4 lamb shanks
Olive oil
1 large onion, roughly chopped
3 carrots, roughly chopped
3 celery sticks, roughly chopped
5 garlic cloves, roughly chopped
3 tbsp tomato purée
250ml port
2 tbsp mint jelly
500ml beef stock
2 sprigs of mint
2 bay leaves
2 sprigs of rosemary
2 sprigs of thyme
1 tbsp cornflour mixed with 2 tbsp cold water
Salt and black pepper

For the mash:
2kg Maris Piper potatoes
250g melted butter

Preheat the oven to 180°C/160°C fan. Season the lamb shanks with salt and pepper and sear them in a large casserole in hot olive oil until browned all over, then lift them out. Add the onion, carrots and celery to the same pan, letting them soften before stirring in the garlic and tomato purée. Cook for a minute, then pour in the port and let it reduce slightly. Stir through the mint jelly, add the beef stock and herbs, then return the lamb shanks to the pan. Put the lid on and cook in the oven for about 3 hours until the meat is tender and falling away from the bone.

Meanwhile, bake the potatoes whole until the skins are crisp and the insides fluffy, about 1½ hours. (If you have two oven compartments, you can speed this up by baking them at 240°C/220°C fan for 50 minutes.) Scoop out the middles, rice or mash them, then stir through the melted butter until smooth and silky. Season with salt.

Once the lamb is ready, lift it out on to a plate and cover with foil. Strain the sauce into a clean pan, reduce it until concentrated and glossy, then stir in a little of the cornflour mixture to thicken to your liking.

Serve a generous spoonful of mash with a lamb shank on top, finished with that rich mint and port gravy poured over.

Roast Beef with Red Wine Gravy

SERVES
4

PREP
10 mins
(+ 1 hour resting)

COOK
30 mins
(+ 20 mins resting)

Of all the roast dinners, roast beef has always been my favourite. There's something special about a joint of beef coming to the table, cooked rare so it's tender, juicy and packed with flavour. With a rich red wine gravy alongside, it's a classic Sunday centrepiece – comforting, impressive and the one I look forward to the most.

1kg beef roasting joint
1½ tbsp Dijon mustard
1½ tbsp olive oil
2 large onions, each cut into 4 thick slices
250ml red wine
2 beef stock cubes dissolved in 400ml boiling water
1 tbsp cornflour mixed with 2 tbsp cold water
Salt and black pepper

Take the beef out of the fridge, pat it dry with kitchen paper and season all over with salt. Leave it at room temperature for 1 hour, then rub the beef all over with the Dijon mustard and black pepper.

Preheat the oven to 200°C/180°C fan. Heat the olive oil in a large frying pan over a high heat, then sear the beef on all sides until well browned. Lay the onion slices in the bottom of a roasting tray and place the beef on top. Roast for about 30 minutes, or until the internal temperature is 50°C for rare. Remove from the oven, cover with foil and rest for 20 minutes until the internal temperature rises to 55–60°C.

While the beef rests, place the roasting tray with the onions over a medium heat on the hob. Pour in the red wine and let it bubble for a minute, scraping up all the browned bits from the bottom of the tray. Stir in the beef stock and simmer for 10 minutes, then add the cornflour mixture and cook, stirring, for an additional 2 minutes until the mixture has thickened and become glossy. Remove the onions at this stage and strain the gravy if you want it smoother. Season to taste.

Carve the beef into thick slices and serve with the red wine gravy and your choice of sides.

Ham, Cheese & Pickle Sandwich with Crisps

SERVES
4

PREP
45
mins
(+ simmering)

COOK
5
hours

Ham, cheese and pickle: it's about as British as it gets. The kind of sandwich you want after a long walk, with a pint by the fire. Slow-cooked pulled gammon glazed with honey and mustard, melty Cheddar and chunky pickle all tucked into a soft white bap. Add a pile of salt and vinegar crisps and it's pub-lunch perfection.

For the gammon:
1.5kg unsmoked gammon joint
1 onion, halved
2 carrots, roughly chopped
2 celery sticks, roughly chopped
8 black peppercorns
3 bay leaves
100g butter
2 tbsp honey
1 tbsp wholegrain mustard
1 tbsp cider vinegar
Zest and juice of ½ lemon

For the chunky pickle:
2 carrots, peeled and diced
1 red onion, diced
1 apple, diced
100ml cider vinegar
1 tbsp golden granulated sugar
1 tbsp dark muscovado sugar
1 tsp ground allspice
1 tbsp Dijon mustard

For the crisps:
4 large Maris Piper potatoes
Vegetable oil, for deep-frying
50ml malt vinegar
1 tsp salt

To assemble:
200g mature Cheddar, grated
4 soft white baps
Butter, for spreading
English mustard, for spreading

Place the gammon in a large pan, cover with cold water and add the onion, carrots, celery, peppercorns and bay leaves. Bring to the boil, skim off any scum, then lower to a gentle simmer and cook for about 4 hours until tender.

Preheat the oven to 200°C/180°C fan. Lift the gammon into a roasting tray and roast in the oven for 10 minutes. Meanwhile, melt the butter in a small pan and stir in the honey, mustard, cider vinegar, lemon zest and juice. Brush this glaze over the gammon and return it to the oven for 20–25 minutes, basting every 5 minutes until sticky and golden. Rest for 10 minutes, then shred the meat in the tray juices.

For the pickle, add all the ingredients to a pan and simmer gently for 15–20 minutes until thickened but still with a bit of bite. Leave to cool slightly, then pulse with a stick blender so it's mainly smooth but still chunky.

For the crisps, peel the potatoes, then slice them thinly on a mandoline. Rinse the slices in cold water and pat dry with a clean tea towel. Half-fill a deep pan with vegetable oil and heat to 170°C, then deep-fry the potato slices (in batches) for 6–8 minutes until golden and crisp. Drain on kitchen paper. Boil the malt vinegar and salt together in a small non-stick pan for 5 minutes until reduced and beginning to crystallise. Once cool, crush into a fine powder and dust over the crisps.

Add the Cheddar to an ovenproof frying pan and slide under a hot grill until bubbling and golden. Split the baps, butter both sides and spread with English mustard. Pile on the pulled gammon, spoon over the melted Cheddar, and top with a generous helping of pickle. Lid on, crisps on the side.

Gammon, Egg & Chips with Spicy Pineapple

SERVES
2

PREP
30
mins
(+ chilling)

COOK
45
mins

Gammon, egg and chips may be more fashionable with your grandparents, but I think it's a belter! Salty gammon with a fried egg on top is already a winning combination, and adding pineapple caramelised with honey and a touch of chilli takes it to the next level. You get that mix of savoury and sweet, with a bit of heat cutting through to keep things interesting, and then of course there are the triple-cooked chips, golden and crisp. It's hearty and familiar.

700g Maris Piper potatoes, peeled and cut into chips
2 litres vegetable oil, for frying
½ pineapple
50g butter
4 tbsp honey
2 tsp chilli flakes
2 gammon steaks
Drizzle of olive oil
2 eggs
Salt and black pepper
English mustard, to serve

Place the potatoes in a bowl of water to rinse off the excess starch, then fill a large pan with cold water, add the chips and bring to a simmer over a medium heat. Cook until the chips are easily pierced with a knife, about 20 minutes. Carefully lift them out, leave to steam dry on a rack, then chill in the fridge.

Heat a deep, heavy-based pan of vegetable oil to 130°C and fry the chips in batches until they form a light crust, about 5 minutes. Remove, drain on a wire rack or kitchen paper, then leave to cool.

Prepare the pineapple by trimming the ends, peeling off the skin and removing any eyes. Slice into thick discs and cut out the core. Melt the butter in a frying pan and brown the pineapple slices on both sides, then add the honey and chilli flakes and cook for a minute more until sticky and caramelised.

Season the gammon steaks with a little salt and some pepper. Heat the drizzle of olive oil in a frying pan over a medium heat and cook the steaks for about 5 minutes on each side until lightly browned and cooked through.

Meanwhile, reheat the oil for the chips to 180°C and fry them again until golden and crisp, about 5–7 minutes. Drain and season with salt. Keep warm in a low oven if needed.

In a separate pan, fry the eggs to your liking. Top the gammon with the pineapple slices and serve with a fried egg on top and the chips on the side. Add English mustard on the side if you fancy it.

Caramelised Red Onion & Mature Cheddar Quiche

SERVES
8

PREP
15
mins

COOK
1
hour

Quiches are one of those things you see everywhere, from family buffets to pub counters, and they've earned their place because of how versatile they are. You can eat them hot or cold, slice them up small for a spread, or serve them as the main event with a bit of salad. This one uses sweet red onions cooked right down with thyme, balanced by plenty of mature Cheddar in a crisp pastry case.

- 1 × 375g sheet of ready-rolled shortcrust pastry
- 3 large red onions, thinly sliced
- 25g butter
- 1 tbsp olive oil
- 4 sprigs of thyme
- 1 tsp soft light brown sugar
- 4 eggs
- 225ml whole milk
- 150ml double cream
- 190g mature Cheddar, grated
- Salt and black pepper

Preheat the oven to 220°C/200°C fan. Unroll the pastry sheet and use it to line a 26–28cm loose-bottomed tart tin, pressing it into the corners. Trim away any very big overhangs of pastry but leave enough so it sits slightly above the rim of the tin. Fold that extra pastry back over the top edge and use your hands to shape it into a neat raised border. Crimp the edge with a fork or flute it with your fingers to finish it off. Prick the base with a fork, line with baking paper and fill with baking beans. Blind bake for 15 minutes, then remove the paper and beans and bake for another 5 minutes until lightly golden. Lower the oven temperature to 200°C/180°C fan.

Meanwhile, cook the red onions with the butter, olive oil and thyme sprigs over a low heat for about 25 minutes, stirring now and then until soft and golden. Add the sugar and cook for a further 5 minutes until caramelised, then lift out the thyme sprigs and set the onions aside to cool slightly.

In a jug, whisk together the eggs, milk, and cream, seasoning with salt and black pepper. Spread the onions over the pastry base, scatter over three-quarters of the Cheddar, then pour in the custard mixture. Top with the remaining cheese.

Bake for 40–45 minutes until the filling is just set and lightly golden on top. Leave to cool for at least 15 minutes before slicing, as this helps it hold together.

Liver & Onions with Creamy Mash & Bacon Crumb

SERVES
2

PREP
15
mins

COOK
40
mins

One of the true traditional classics of British cooking. It's gone out of fashion a bit over the years, but I think it's absolutely delicious. I've added a splash of ale for extra flavour and a crispy smoked bacon crumb on top for a bit of indulgence and texture.

15g butter
1 tbsp olive oil, plus a drizzle
1 large onion, thinly sliced
1 tbsp plain flour, plus extra seasoned flour for dusting
100ml real ale
150ml beef stock
1 tsp Worcestershire sauce
100g smoked streaky bacon
300g lamb's liver, trimmed and sliced
Salt and black pepper

For the mash:
500g floury potatoes, peeled and cut into chunks
40g butter, melted
Splash of milk

For the mash, bring a large pan of salted water to the boil and cook the potatoes until soft, about 15 minutes. Drain well, then mash until smooth. Stir through the melted butter and splash of milk until creamy, then season to taste.

While the potatoes cook, heat the butter and tablespoon of oil in a large frying pan over a medium heat. Add the onion and cook gently for 15–20 minutes until soft and golden. Stir in the tablespoon of flour and cook for a minute before pouring in the ale. Let it bubble for a minute or two, then add the beef stock and Worcestershire sauce. Season with salt and pepper, then leave to simmer gently until thickened.

In another pan, fry the smoked streaky bacon until crisp, then transfer to kitchen paper and finely chop into a crumb for later.

Dust the liver slices lightly in seasoned flour. Using the same pan, heat a drizzle of oil over a medium-high heat and fry the liver for 1–2 minutes on each side until browned but still slightly pink in the middle. Transfer to the pan of onion gravy and let it rest off the heat for a few minutes so everything comes together.

Serve generous spoonfuls of mash topped with the liver and rich onion gravy, then scatter over the crispy smoked bacon crumb to finish.

Steak & Chips with Whisky Peppercorn Sauce

SERVES
2

PREP
45
mins
(+ 2 hours seasoning)

COOK
1
hour

Steak and chips might sound simple, but when done right, with high-quality ingredients, it becomes something special. Golden, crunchy chips cooked three times for the perfect bite, a well-seasoned sirloin steak basted in butter, garlic and herbs, and then a sauce that is rich with cream and whisky, lifted by the sharp pop of green peppercorns. It is straightforward pub food made luxurious and indulgent without being fussy – the kind of dish that hits the spot all year round.

---

2 thick sirloin steaks
3 large Maris Piper potatoes, peeled and cut into thick chips
2 litres vegetable oil, for frying
1 tbsp beef dripping
1 tbsp butter
1 garlic clove, crushed
2 sprigs of rosemary
2 sprigs of thyme
Sea salt and black pepper

For the whisky peppercorn sauce:
1 tbsp black peppercorns
3 tbsp butter
1 shallot, finely diced
1 garlic clove, finely chopped
1 tbsp thyme leaves, finely chopped
50ml whisky
3 tbsp green peppercorns
200ml beef stock
100ml double cream
1 tbsp red wine vinegar

Season the steaks with salt and leave them in the fridge for a couple of hours.

Rinse the starch off the potatoes, add them to a pan of salted water, bring to the boil and simmer until just tender. Drain, spread out on a tray and chill in the fridge for 30 minutes. Heat the vegetable oil in a large pan to 130°C and fry the chips for 5–6 minutes until a light crust forms, then drain and chill again. Increase the temperature of the oil to 180°C and fry the chips a final time until golden and crisp, then season with sea salt.

Heat the beef dripping in a frying pan over a high heat, add the steaks and sear for 3–4 minutes on each side for medium (or to your liking). Add the butter, garlic, rosemary and thyme sprigs and baste the steaks as they finish cooking. Remove the steaks from the pan and rest for 5–10 minutes while you make the sauce.

Crush the black peppercorns with a pestle and mortar. Melt 2 tablespoons of the butter in the same pan used for the steaks, add the crushed peppercorns and fry for 30 seconds to release their oils. Add the shallot and garlic and cook until softened. Stir in the thyme, add the whisky and carefully set alight to burn off the alcohol. Add the green peppercorns and beef stock and reduce by half. Lower the heat, stir in the cream and vinegar and simmer until thick enough to coat the back of a spoon, then finish with the remaining butter.

Slice the steaks, plate them up with the triple-cooked chips, and spoon over the whisky peppercorn sauce.

Chapter Three

THINGS ON TOAST

Spicy Prawn Cocktail on Sourdough with Bloody Mary Dressing

SERVES
2

PREP
15
mins

COOK
5
mins

I love a good prawn cocktail. It's nostalgic, a bit retro and makes for a lighter choice when you don't fancy anything too heavy. I've always been partial to a Bloody Mary too, especially after a big night, so bringing those flavours together just wins for me. The vodka and Tabasco cut through the richness of the sauce, and piling it all on to toast gives it that laid-back, pub-lunch feel. Add some smashed avocado, fresh and crunchy salad and a dusting of cayenne to finish; it's everything I want from a brunch dish with a bit of attitude.

200g cooked king prawns, peeled
1 spring onion
2 thick slices of granary or sourdough bread
Butter, for spreading
1 avocado
1 tomato, thinly sliced
¼ cucumber, thinly sliced
1 small gem lettuce, shredded
Cayenne pepper, for dusting

For the Bloody Mary dressing:
50g mayonnaise
50g tomato ketchup
1 tbsp vodka
1 tbsp Worcestershire sauce
1 tsp Tabasco
Juice of ½ lemon
Salt and black pepper

Start by making the Bloody Mary dressing. In a bowl, mix the mayo, ketchup, vodka, Worcestershire sauce, Tabasco and lemon juice until smooth. Season well with salt and pepper, then fold in the prawns so they're nicely coated. Chill in the fridge while you prep everything else.

Slice the spring onion into thin strips and pop them into a small bowl of iced water to help them curl up.

Toast your bread slices and butter them while they're warm. Peel and de-stone the avocado, smash with a fork and season with some salt, then spread it over the toast.

Top with the sliced tomato and cucumber, followed by a generous handful of shredded lettuce.

Spoon the prawns and sauce on top, letting the sauce dribble slightly over the sides. Drain the spring onions and scatter over the top, then finish with a light dusting of cayenne pepper.

Welsh Rarebit

SERVES
2

PREP
10
mins

COOK
10
mins

Welsh rarebit is comfort food through and through. We went on a cruise years ago for a mate's wedding, and after a night in Le Club, there was only one place still open to eat. On the late-night menu sat Welsh rarebit and it went down a storm after a few drinks. The molten cheese with the kick of mustard and Tabasco makes it rich, savoury and hard to resist.

---

2 thick slices of sourdough bread
20g salted butter
20g plain flour
120ml ale
1 tsp English mustard
½ tsp smoked paprika
1–2 dashes of Tabasco
150g extra-mature Cheddar, grated
1 egg yolk
Black pepper

Toast the sourdough on both sides under a hot grill until golden, then set aside. Melt the butter in a pan over a medium heat. Stir in the flour and cook for a couple of minutes to form a roux, then slowly whisk in the ale until smooth and thickened.

Stir through the mustard, smoked paprika and Tabasco, then take the pan off the heat and add the cheese, mixing until melted and glossy. Beat in the egg yolk and season with black pepper.

Lay the toast on a baking tray, spoon the mixture generously over each slice and spread it right to the edges so they don't burn. Place back under the grill until bubbling and bronzed on top.

Garlic Butter Sardines on Toast with Lemon Zest & Cottage Cheese

SERVES
2

PREP
20
mins
(+ 20 mins pickling)

COOK
10
mins

Sardines fried gently in butter with garlic, lemon and capers, laid over toasted sourdough spread with smooth lemon-and-dill cottage cheese with horseradish cream and cucumber. Topped with pickled red onion and parsley – this is rich, fresh and full of contrast.

½ red onion, thinly sliced
50ml white wine vinegar
½ tsp golden granulated sugar
125g cottage cheese
Zest of ½ lemon, plus juice of ¼ lemon
Small handful of fresh dill, finely chopped
¼ cucumber, coarsely grated, salted and squeezed of excess water
2 tsp horseradish cream (or to taste)
25g butter
6 small tinned sardine fillets in olive oil
1 small garlic clove, thinly sliced
2 tsp capers, drained
2 thick slices of sourdough bread
Small handful of flat-leaf parsley, finely chopped
Salt and black pepper

Put the onion into a small bowl. Warm the vinegar with the sugar and a pinch of salt until the sugar dissolves, then pour over the onion. Leave to pickle for at least 20 minutes.

Blend the cottage cheese with the lemon zest, dill and some salt and pepper until smooth. Stir through the drained cucumber and horseradish cream, taste and adjust the seasoning, then keep chilled until ready to serve.

Melt the butter in a frying pan over a medium heat. Add the sardines and fry gently for 1–2 minutes until warmed and starting to crisp. Add the garlic and cook briefly without browning, then squeeze in the lemon juice and stir through the capers. Let everything sizzle together for a few seconds before tossing to coat.

Toast the sourdough until golden. While still warm, spoon over a generous layer of the cottage cheese mixture and spread right to the edges. Top with three sardine fillets per slice, spoon over some of the lemon and caper butter from the pan, then finish with the drained pickled onion and a scatter of parsley. Serve straight away while the sardines are hot and the cheese is cool underneath.

Chilli Marmite Mushrooms on Sourdough

SERVES
2

PREP
10
mins

COOK
15
mins

This is one of those quick and easy dishes that works just as well for a weekday lunch as it does for a weekend brunch. The mushrooms are cooked down in butter with garlic, a little chilli and Marmite until they're sticky, savoury and full of flavour. Spread some cream cheese on toasted sourdough, pile the mushrooms high and finish with parsley and a pinch of chilli flakes. Simple, satisfying and ready in no time.

2 tbsp butter
2 garlic cloves, finely chopped
1 red chilli, finely chopped
250g chestnut mushrooms, thickly sliced
2 tsp Marmite
2 tbsp water
Zest and juice of ½ lemon
2 slices of sourdough bread
2 tbsp cream cheese
Small handful of parsley, chopped
Pinch of chilli flakes

Melt the butter in a frying pan over a low-medium heat. Add the garlic and red chilli and cook gently for 1–2 minutes until soft and fragrant. Turn up the heat slightly, add the mushrooms and fry for 5–6 minutes until golden and tender.

Stir in the Marmite with a splash of water and let it bubble down until the mushrooms are sticky and glossy. Squeeze over the lemon juice and mix well.

Toast the sourdough, spread with the cream cheese, then spoon the mushrooms generously over the top. Finish with parsley, chilli flakes and a scattering of lemon zest before serving.

Black Pudding & Apple on Toast with Fried Egg

SERVES
2

PREP
10
mins

COOK
15
mins

Black pudding is one of those ingredients people either love or hate; I'm firmly on the love side. It's great to see it getting the respect it deserves on pub menus these days, not just as a breakfast side but as the star of the show. The richness of the pudding, the sweetness from the apple and that golden runny yolk on top make this a cracking pub-style brunch or snack. Simple steps but loads of flavour.

200g black pudding
Butter or oil for frying, plus butter for spreading
1 apple, diced into 1cm cubes
2 spring onions, thinly sliced
1 tsp honey
2 eggs
2 slices of sourdough bread
Salt and black pepper
Hot sauce, to serve

Cut the black pudding into chunky 2cm cubes and fry in a little butter or oil over a medium heat until crisp on the outside. Season with salt and pepper, then remove from the pan. Add a touch more butter or oil if needed, then add the diced apple and spring onions and fry for a few minutes until softened and golden. Drizzle in the honey and season lightly.

In a separate pan, fry the eggs to your liking. Toast and butter the sourdough, then pile on the crispy black pudding, top with the fried egg, and scatter over the warm apple and spring onion mix. If you like things saucy, like me, finish with a drizzle of your favourite hot sauce.

Roast Butternut & Goat's Cheese on Toast with Pumpkin Seeds

SERVES
4

PREP
15
mins

COOK
40
mins

Long roasted slices of butternut squash layered over a rich goat's cheese spread, finished with pumpkin seeds, chilli flakes and sea salt. A great little brunch idea that's a bit different – simple to make but feels like something you'd order out.

---

1 large butternut squash (about 1.2kg), peeled, deseeded and cut into long, 1cm-thick slices
3 tbsp olive oil, plus extra for drizzling
1 tsp honey
1 tsp dried thyme
40g pumpkin seeds, toasted in a dry pan
300g soft goat's cheese
4 tbsp crème fraîche
4 thick slices of sourdough bread
1 garlic clove, cut in half
Pinch of chilli flakes
Sea salt flakes and black pepper

Preheat the oven to 220°C/200°C fan. Lay the squash slices on a tray, drizzle with 2 tablespoons of the olive oil and the honey, sprinkle with thyme, salt and pepper, then roast for 30–35 minutes until golden and tender, turning halfway.

Toast the pumpkin seeds in a dry pan until they pop, then set aside.

Mix the goat's cheese with the crème fraîche, the remaining tablespoon of olive oil and some salt and pepper until smooth and spreadable.

Toast the sourdough, then rub with the cut side of the garlic. Spread a thick layer of the cheese mixture over each slice, arrange the roasted squash slices on top and finish with the pumpkin seeds, a drizzle of olive oil, a pinch of chilli flakes and some sea salt flakes.

Buttery Scrambled Eggs with Hot Honey & Crispy Sweetcorn

SERVES
2

PREP
10
mins

COOK
25
mins

Soft, rich scrambled eggs that melt in the mouth are cooked with some Cheddar for extra creaminess, then paired with sweetcorn roasted until golden and crunchy for a bit of texture. The drizzle of hot honey brings a sweet heat that cuts through the richness and ties it all together. Finished with chives and a sprinkle of chilli flakes, it's the kind of brunch dish that feels a little indulgent but is still simple to put together at home.

150g sweetcorn (fresh or drained from a tin)
1 tsp olive oil
½ tsp hot paprika
4 eggs
25ml milk
20g butter, plus extra for spreading
30g mature Cheddar, grated
2 slices sourdough
1 tbsp hot honey
1 tbsp chopped chives
Pinch of chilli flakes
Salt and black pepper

Preheat the oven to 200°C/180°C fan. Drain the sweetcorn well, pat dry with kitchen paper, then toss with olive oil, paprika and a little salt. Spread out on a baking tray and roast in the oven for 20–25 minutes until golden and crisp.

Meanwhile, whisk the eggs with the milk and season lightly. In a pan, melt the butter gently, pour in the eggs and stir slowly over a low heat. As they begin to thicken, stir in the grated Cheddar and continue to gently move the eggs with a spatula to keep them creamy and soft. Once just set but still glossy, take off the heat.

Toast the sourdough slices and butter them generously. Spoon the scrambled eggs on to the toast, scatter over the crispy sweetcorn and drizzle with hot honey. Finish with chopped chives and a pinch of chilli flakes before serving.

● **Cost-saving tip:** *You can make your own hot honey by warming 60g honey with 1 tsp cider vinegar, ½ tsp chilli flakes and a pinch of chilli powder for 2–3 minutes until infused. Leave to cool.*

Curried Egg Mayo on Toasted White with Crispy Onions

SERVES
2

PREP
20
mins

COOK
15
mins

Egg mayonnaise sandwiches have always been one of those simple pleasures: a buffet staple and a sandwich that's perfect for a picnic. This version retains the comforting base but elevates it with a spoonful of curry paste for warmth and spice, then finishes with a layer of homemade crispy onions for extra crunch and a scattering of chives for freshness. Served open on toasted thick-cut white bread; it feels familiar yet with a bit of character.

4 eggs
60g mayonnaise
1 tbsp curry paste (your favourite)
1 tbsp plain flour
1 tbsp cornflour
1 small onion, very thinly sliced
Vegetable oil, for frying
2 slices of thick-cut white bread
20g butter, softened
Small bunch of chives, finely chopped
Salt and black pepper

Put the eggs in a pan of cold water, bring to the boil and cook for 8 minutes. Drain and cool under running water, then peel and roughly chop. Mix with the mayonnaise, curry paste and a little salt and black pepper until smooth and creamy.

For the crispy onions, mix the plain flour and cornflour and toss the sliced onion through until well coated. Heat a shallow layer of vegetable oil in a frying pan until hot, then fry the onion in small batches until golden and crisp. Drain on kitchen paper and season lightly with salt.

Toast the bread and spread it with the butter. Pile the curried egg mayo on to each slice, top with the crispy onions and finish with some chopped chives. Serve immediately while the toast is crisp and the onions are crunchy.

Coronation Chicken on Toast with Watercress

SERVES
2

PREP
15
mins

COOK
25
mins

I made coronation chicken in my first food tech class in Year 7 – or more accurately, I assembled it. The night before, my dad mixed the mayonnaise with curry paste, chopped the salad, cut and buttered the bread – he basically did the lot. All I had to do at school was put it all together and hope for the best. Let's just say my teacher wasn't too impressed. This version's got a bit more going on – warm, on toast, with spiced yoghurt dressing, almond flakes and dressed watercress to lift it.

300g chicken breast
1 garlic clove, finely grated
1 knob of fresh ginger, peeled and finely grated
1 lemon, ½ cut into slices
1 tbsp tikka or rogan josh curry paste
50g mayonnaise
100g Greek yoghurt
1 tbsp mango chutney
1 tbsp sultanas, finely chopped
½ small red onion, very thinly sliced
2 thick slices of sourdough
30g butter, for the toast
50g watercress
1 tsp olive oil
Salt and black pepper
2 tbsp toasted flaked almonds, to garnish

Preheat the oven to 200°C/180°C fan. Wrap the chicken in foil with the garlic, ginger, lemon slices and a pinch of salt and pepper. Bake for 25 minutes until cooked through. Let it rest for a few minutes, remove the slices of lemon, then shred the chicken with two forks.

In a bowl, mix the curry paste, mayonnaise, yoghurt, mango chutney, chopped sultanas, red onion and the juice from the other half of the lemon. Add the shredded chicken and stir until everything's well coated.

Toast the bread, and butter the slices while still hot. Toss the watercress with the olive oil and a pinch of salt and pepper.

Add the dressed watercress to the toast, then pile on the coronation chicken. Finish by sprinkling over the flaked almonds.

- **Time-saving tip:** *Grab some cooked chicken from the supermarket – it will still taste great!*

Sausage & Cheese Toast

SERVES
2

PREP
5
mins

COOK
10
mins

Sausage and cheese on toast isn't groundbreaking, but this version has been one of the most popular things I've shared on my social channels, and many of you tried it at home. Crispy sausage cooked straight on to the bread, sharp Cheddar, a hit of Dijon and a splash of Worcestershire sauce – perfect for a weekend morning when you want something easy and full of flavour.

---

2 slices of crusty granary bread
4 small or 2 large sausages
Olive oil, for frying
1 tbsp Dijon mustard
100g mature Cheddar, grated
1 tbsp Worcestershire sauce
Chutney, to serve

Lightly toast your bread while you remove the sausage meat from the skins. Mash it straight on to the lightly toasted bread – like you would an avocado – pressing it right to the edges so it sticks. Heat a splash of olive oil in a pan and lay the toast meat-side down. Cook for about 5–6 minutes until the sausage is fully cooked and caramelised underneath.

Lift the slices out and spread the Dijon mustard across the cooked sausage side. Sprinkle the grated cheese over the mixture and drizzle with Worcestershire sauce. Slide them under a hot grill until the cheese is melted, golden and bubbling.

Serve hot, with a dollop of chutney on the side.

Tomatoes & Mackerel on Toast with Herby Caper Oil

SERVES
4

PREP
10
mins

COOK
15
mins

Mackerel on toast is something my brother and sister and I have eaten since we were kids, the tins in tomato sauce, mashed with a splash of vinegar on toast. Not your everyday dish, maybe, but it always has been in our house. Here, it's elevated into something fresh and summery, featuring crisp-skinned fillets, sweet cherry tomatoes and a punchy herby caper oil.

2 tbsp olive oil, plus extra for frying
4 mackerel fillets, skin on
300g cherry tomatoes
2 garlic cloves, thinly sliced
1 tsp red wine vinegar
4 thick slices of sourdough
Salt and black pepper

For the herby caper oil:
2 tbsp capers, drained
10g fresh basil leaves
10g fresh parsley leaves
3 tbsp olive oil
1 tbsp lemon juice
1 tsp wholegrain mustard

Heat a splash of olive oil in a large frying pan and lay in the mackerel fillets, skin-side down. Cook for 3–4 minutes until the skin is golden and crisp, then lift the fillets out on to a plate without flipping them.

To the same pan, add the cherry tomatoes, garlic, 2 tablespoons olive oil and some salt and pepper. Cook gently over a medium heat until the tomatoes soften but still hold their shape, then splash in the red wine vinegar. Let it bubble down slightly until the juices turn saucy but the tomatoes remain intact.

For the herby caper oil, blitz or finely chop the capers, basil and parsley, then stir through the olive oil, lemon juice and wholegrain mustard. Season with salt and pepper.

Toast the sourdough until golden, then spoon the tomatoes and their juices over it. Lay the mackerel on top, drizzle generously with the herby caper oil and serve straight away.

Chapter Four

PROPER PIES

Fish Pie with Smoked Cheddar Cream Sauce

SERVES
6–8

PREP
35
mins

COOK
50
mins

My mum used to have fish pie on the weekly rotation in our house, and for me it's one of those meals that feels like home. Creamy, rich and comforting, it's the kind of meal that brings everyone round the table and leaves you going back for seconds. This version is lifted with smoked Cheddar, fennel and gherkins for a little tang, while the dill and parsley bring it all together with freshness. Perfect family food that feels indulgent but comforting at the same time.

50g butter
2 shallots, finely diced
1 small fennel bulb, thinly sliced
2 leeks, thinly sliced
50g plain flour
400ml double cream
75g smoked Cheddar, grated
350g cod, cut into chunks
300g prawns, peeled and deveined
350g salmon, cut into chunks
100g frozen peas
2 tbsp chopped parsley, plus extra to garnish
2 tbsp chopped dill
3 gherkins, finely chopped
Juice of 1 lemon

For the potato topping:
1.5kg Maris Piper potatoes, peeled and diced
75g butter
3 egg yolks
Salt and black pepper

First prepare the potato topping. Boil the potatoes in salted water for 15–20 minutes until tender. Drain and mash until smooth, then mix in the butter, egg yolks and seasoning. Set aside.

Melt the butter in a large pan over a medium heat, then add the shallots, fennel and leeks. Cook for 5–7 minutes until softened, season, then stir in the flour and cook for 1–2 minutes. Gradually pour in the cream while stirring to form a smooth sauce. Stir in the smoked Cheddar until melted.

Fold in the cod, prawns, salmon, peas, parsley, dill, gherkins and lemon juice. Taste and adjust the seasoning. Cook gently for 2–3 minutes, allowing the fish to begin cooking through while remaining tender. Meanwhile, preheat the oven to 220°C/200°C fan.

Spoon the fish mixture into a large ovenproof dish and spread the mashed potato evenly over the top, fluffing the surface with a fork. Bake for 25–30 minutes until the top is golden and the filling is bubbling. Leave to rest for 5 minutes, then sprinkle with chopped parsley to serve.

- **Cost-saving tip:** *Swap some of the salmon and prawns for extra white fish such as pollock or coley – it still makes a fantastic pie while keeping the price down.*

Chicken, Leek & Bacon Pie with Mash & Gravy

SERVES
4

PREP
40
mins

COOK
1 hr 20
mins

A hearty, comforting pie with buttery mash on the side, this is the kind of food that makes me think of pub menus in the colder months. Smoky bacon, tender chicken and sweet leeks wrapped up in crisp pastry, finished with a gravy that's lifted by a touch of orange. Rich, warming and just the sort of dish you want when you're after something filling but a little bit special.

---

2 tbsp olive oil
600g chicken thigh fillets, diced
150g smoked streaky bacon, chopped
1 white onion, finely chopped
2 garlic cloves, finely chopped
2 large leeks, sliced
50g butter
2 tbsp plain flour
300ml chicken stock
2 tbsp chopped parsley
1 tbsp chopped tarragon
1 tbsp Dijon mustard
700–800g ready-made shortcrust pastry
1 egg yolk, beaten
Salt and black pepper

For the gravy:
1 tbsp olive oil
50g butter
2 shallots, finely chopped
2 garlic cloves, finely chopped
1 tsp orange zest
Juice of 1 orange
150ml white wine
300ml chicken stock
1 tsp Worcestershire sauce
2 tsp cornflour mixed with 2 tsp water

For the mash:
800g potatoes, peeled and quartered
200g butter
150ml whole milk

- **Time-saving tip:** *Make the filling the day before and keep it chilled – not only does it save time on the day, but it also helps the flavours develop, and the pastry base stays crisp when baking.*

Heat 1 tablespoon of the oil in a large pan, season the chicken pieces and brown them all over before lifting them out on to a plate. Add the bacon and fry until crispy, then remove from the pan. Heat the final tablespoon of oil in the same pan, then add the onion and garlic with a pinch of seasoning, cook until softened, then stir in the leeks and cook gently until soft. Return the bacon to the pan.

In a separate pan, melt the butter, stir in the flour and cook for a minute to make a roux. Gradually whisk in the stock until you've got a smooth, thick sauce. Stir through the parsley, tarragon and mustard, then fold in the chicken and bacon–leek mixture. Leave to cool slightly.

Preheat the oven to 210°C/190°C fan. Roll out two-thirds of the shortcrust pastry and line the pie dish, leaving some overhang. Place the pastry in the fridge for 30 minutes, or in the freezer for 10–15 minutes, just to help it keep its shape. Prick the pastry base with a fork, line with baking paper and fill with baking beans. Blind bake for 20 minutes, then remove the beans and paper and bake for an additional 5 minutes, until lightly golden. Leave to cool slightly. Spoon in the chicken filling, lay the remaining pastry on top and crimp and trim the edges. Brush with egg yolk and bake for 35 minutes until golden.

For the gravy, heat the oil and half the butter in a pan and soften the shallots and garlic. Add the orange zest and juice with the wine and let it bubble and reduce. Pour in the stock, stir through the Worcestershire sauce and thicken with the cornflour mixture. Finish with the remaining butter for gloss.

For the mash, boil the potatoes in salted water until tender, then drain and mash with the butter and milk until smooth and creamy. Season to taste.

Serve generous slices of pie with the mashed potatoes on the side and plenty of the gravy poured over.

Butter Chicken Pie with Naan Lid

SERVES
6–8

PREP
50 mins
(+ 1 hour proving and marinating)

COOK
1 hr 20 mins

This one's a little different, but that's what makes it so good. The butter chicken sauce is rich and full of flavour, and the naan lid gives you the perfect way to mop it all up. Breaking through the bread and letting it soak up that sauce is exactly what this dish is all about. It's comforting, indulgent and brings two classics together in a fun way. It's the kind of dish that pairs beautifully with a crisp, cold lager – comfort food with a twist.

---

4 tbsp tandoori masala
5 tsp freshly grated ginger
5 tsp freshly grated garlic
240g natural yoghurt
2 tbsp oil
1kg boneless chicken breast
4 tbsp ghee
4 large onions, thinly sliced
2 tbsp tomato purée
2 × 400g tins chopped tomatoes
2 tsp chilli powder
3 tsp ground coriander
3 tsp ground cumin
240ml double cream
1 tsp garam masala
Salt and black pepper

For the naan:
7g fast-action yeast
¾ tsp sugar
240ml warm water
400g strong white bread flour
3 tbsp natural yoghurt
1½ tbsp melted butter, plus extra for brushing
¾ tsp salt
1½ tsp nigella (onion) seeds
1 garlic clove, finely grated
2 tbsp finely chopped fresh coriander

Mix the tandoori masala, 2 teaspoons of the grated ginger, 2 teaspoons of the grated garlic, the yoghurt and oil in a bowl, season lightly, then add the chicken and stir to coat. Leave to marinate for at least 30 minutes or, ideally, overnight in the fridge.

Heat the ghee in a deep pan and add the onions with a pinch of salt. Cook gently until golden and soft, about 10 minutes. Stir in the remaining grated ginger and garlic and cook for a minute, then add the tomato purée and fry for another minute to deepen the flavour. Add the chopped tomatoes, chilli powder, ground coriander and cumin. Simmer for 5 minutes, adding a splash of water if it gets too thick, then take off the heat and blend until smooth.

Grill or griddle the marinated chicken until cooked through and lightly charred, then cut into 3cm chunks. Add the cream and garam masala to the blended sauce, bring to a gentle simmer, then add the chicken and stir through. Set aside.

For the naan, stir the yeast and sugar into the warm water and leave for 10 minutes until frothy. In a large bowl, mix the flour, yoghurt and melted butter, then pour in the yeast mixture. Mix to a dough, then add the salt. Knead for 8–10 minutes until smooth, cover, and leave to prove for 1 hour, or until doubled in size. Knock back the dough and roll it out to just larger than your pie dish. Scatter the nigella seeds over the surface, pressing them lightly into the surface.

Preheat the oven to 220°C/200°C fan. Spoon the butter chicken into a large pie dish (or two medium ones). Lay the naan dough over the top with a 2–3cm overhang, press it firmly to the rim of the dish to seal, and trim or fold in the edges. Lightly brush with butter before baking. Bake for 25–30 minutes until the bread is puffed up and golden.

Melt a little butter with the grated garlic and chopped coriander, then brush generously over the hot naan lid as soon as the pie comes out of the oven.

Cheese & Onion Pie with Smoky Baked Beans

SERVES
6–8

PREP
45 mins

COOK
1 hr 10 mins

This pie takes inspiration from the cheese and onion pies my mum makes at our family's chip shop. For me, it was always with chips and beans – absolute comfort and a combination that still feels unbeatable on a cold day, which is quite common here in Buxton. Slow-cooked onions, plenty of strong cheese and crisp shortcrust pastry, baked until golden and sliceable. The smoky baked beans bring a bit of tang and spice that cuts through the richness, turning this into a plate that's as homely as it gets.

700–800g ready-made shortcrust pastry
40g butter
1 tbsp olive oil
1.2kg white onions (about 5 large), thinly sliced
1 tsp salt
1 tsp white pepper
2 tsp Worcestershire sauce
1 tbsp English mustard
300g extra-mature Cheddar, grated
200g Red Leicester, grated
1 egg yolk, beaten with a splash of milk
Chips, to serve

For the smoky baked beans:
2 tbsp olive oil
2 shallots, finely chopped
2 garlic cloves, finely chopped
2 tsp smoked paprika
4 tbsp chipotle paste
4 tbsp red wine vinegar
2 x 400g tins chopped tomatoes
2 tsp sugar
1 beef stock cube
2 tsp salt
4 × 400g tins cannellini beans, drained and rinsed

Preheat the oven to 200°C/180°C fan. Roll out two-thirds of the shortcrust and line a 30cm shallow pie dish, leaving some overhang. Prick the base with a fork, line with baking paper and fill with baking beans. Blind bake for 20 minutes, then remove the paper and beans and bake for an additional 5 minutes, until lightly golden. Leave to cool slightly. Place the pastry in the fridge for 30 minutes, or in the freezer for 10–15 minutes, just to help it keep its shape.

Heat the butter and olive oil in a large pan, then add the onions, salt, white pepper and Worcestershire sauce. Cook gently for 25–30 minutes until soft and golden. Stir in the mustard, then fold through the cheeses until you've got a thick, rich filling. Let it cool a little.

Spoon the mixture into the pastry case and smooth it out evenly. Roll out the remaining shortcrust and lay it over the top, sealing with the edges of the base. Trim, crimp and cut a couple of steam holes, then brush with the egg glaze. Bake for 35–40 minutes until the pastry is golden brown and crisp. Leave to rest for 15 minutes before slicing.

For the beans, heat the olive oil in a pan and gently cook the shallots and garlic for 5 minutes until softened. Stir in the smoked paprika, chipotle paste and vinegar, letting it sizzle for a minute. Add the tomatoes, sugar, stock cube and salt, then simmer for 10 minutes until slightly thickened. Stir in the beans and cook for an additional 15 minutes until the sauce is rich and glossy.

Serve big slices of the pie with chips and a ladle of smoky beans for the kind of comfort food that never goes out of fashion.

PIE

Traditional Pork Pie with Chunky Pickle

SERVES
6–8

PREP
1 hour
(+ cooling and chilling)

COOK
2¼ hours

Pork pie has to be one of my favourites: perfect on its own, tucked into a picnic, or brought out at family gatherings, it always feels special, especially at Christmas. Thickly sliced with a spoonful of pickle and a good smear of mustard – it's a belter. The seasoning in the filling and the richness of the pastry give it a comforting depth of flavour, and because this is a large pie, it's ideal to bring out as a showpiece for a big occasion. The sharp, spiced pickle on the side complements the dish perfectly.

For the hot water crust pastry:
210ml water
165g lard
1½ tsp salt
525g plain flour, sifted
1 egg yolk, beaten

For the filling and jelly:
750g pork shoulder, very finely diced
150g smoked bacon, very finely chopped
1½ tsp ground nutmeg (or about ¾ whole nutmeg, freshly grated)
1½ tsp ground coriander
1½ tsp chicken stock powder
1½ tsp salt
1½ tsp black pepper
450ml chicken stock
18g powdered gelatine (or about 9 standard leaves, 1.8–2g each)

Cost-saving tip: *Buy a pork shoulder and dice it yourself rather than using pre-cut packs. Bacon offcuts from the butcher also work well as an alternative to smoked rashers.*

Start with the pastry. Heat the water, lard and salt together in a pan until just boiling. Tip the flour into a large bowl, then pour in the hot liquid and stir until the mixture comes together. Knead lightly until smooth, then cover and keep warm.

Mix the very finely diced pork shoulder and bacon with the nutmeg, coriander, chicken stock powder, salt and black pepper until everything is well combined. Preheat the oven to 200°C/180°C fan.

Take two-thirds of the pastry and roll it out while still warm to a thickness of about 6–8mm, then use it to line a greased deep 18–20cm springform tin, pressing the pastry firmly into the corners and up the sides with an overhang. Pack in the pork mixture, pressing down to avoid any air pockets. Roll out the remaining pastry for the lid, lay it over, and crimp the edges firmly to seal – ensure the crimp is tight so that no liquid can escape during cooking or when the jelly is added later. Make a steam hole in the centre using the handle end of a wooden spoon. Brush the top with the beaten egg yolk.

Bake in the oven for 30 minutes, then reduce the temperature to 180°C/160°C fan and bake for a further 1½ hours. Remove from the oven and let the pie cool slightly so you don't burn yourself. Then, using tea towels to hold the tin, place your thumbs gently on the lid to keep it in place. Carefully tilt the pie over a bowl and pour out any excess juices through the steam hole. Work slowly so the pastry stays intact.

For the chunky pickle:
2 carrots, peeled and diced
1 red onion, diced
1 apple, diced
100ml cider vinegar
1 tbsp golden granulated sugar
1 tbsp dark muscovado sugar
1 tsp ground allspice
1 tbsp Dijon mustard, plus extra to serve

● **Time-saving tips:** *The pickle can be made up to 3 days ahead and kept in the fridge – the flavours improve as it sits. The pastry can also be made the night before and gently warmed before rolling out. You can also pulse the pork shoulder in a food processor, if you don't want to dice it by hand.*

For the jelly, bring the chicken stock up to a gentle simmer in a pan, then remove from the heat. If using powdered gelatine, sprinkle it evenly over the hot stock and whisk until fully dissolved. If using leaves, soak them in cold water for 5 minutes, then squeeze out the excess water and stir them into the hot stock until they are melted. Allow the liquid to cool until just warm. Using a small funnel, pour the jelly into the pie through the steam hole in stages, letting it settle each time before adding more. Chill the pie overnight to allow the jelly to set fully before slicing.

For the pickle, combine the carrots, onion, apple, cider vinegar, both sugars, allspice and Dijon mustard in a pan. Simmer over a medium heat for 15–20 minutes until the sauce has thickened but the veg still retains a bit of bite. Cool slightly, then pulse with a stick blender just enough to smooth it out while leaving some chunks for texture.

Serve thick slices of the cold pork pie, accompanied by a generous spoonful of chunky pickle and a dollop of mustard on the side.

Shepherd's Pie with Rosemary Mash

SERVES
6–8

PREP
25
mins

COOK
1
hour

This is one of those timeless comfort dishes – hearty, warming and deeply satisfying. This version takes the midweek special up a notch with red wine in the filling, and Parmesan and Cheddar in the mash, giving it richness and depth. The rosemary brings a gentle earthiness, and finishing it off with a golden crust makes it a great dish to put down in the middle of the table for everyone to tuck into.

---

2 tbsp olive oil
1kg lamb mince
1 large onion, diced
1 large carrot, diced
1 celery stick, diced
2 garlic cloves, finely chopped
2 tbsp Worcestershire sauce
1½ tbsp tomato purée
2 sprigs of fresh thyme, leaves finely chopped
1 sprig of fresh rosemary, leaves finely chopped
250ml red wine
250ml chicken stock
Salt and black pepper

For the potato topping:
2kg Maris Piper potatoes, peeled and cut into chunks
4 tbsp butter
100g Cheddar, grated
60ml double cream
2 egg yolks
2 sprigs of fresh rosemary, leaves finely chopped
7 tbsp grated Parmesan

Preheat the oven to 200°C/180°C fan. Heat the oil in a large pan, season the lamb mince, and cook over a medium-high heat for 2–3 minutes until browned. Stir in the onion, carrot, celery and garlic, then mix in the Worcestershire sauce, tomato purée, thyme and rosemary and cook for another couple of minutes. Pour in the red wine, let it reduce until almost gone, then add the stock. Simmer until thickened, then season.

Boil the potatoes in salted water until tender, then drain and return to the pan briefly to dry out. Mash with the butter, Cheddar, cream, egg yolks and rosemary, seasoning to taste.

Spread the lamb mixture in an ovenproof dish and top with the mash, fluffing the surface with a fork. Sprinkle with the Parmesan, season and bake for 20 minutes, until golden and bubbling.

● **Time-saving tip:** *This dish is ideal for meal prep – make a significant portion, split it into containers and freeze. It reheats brilliantly and makes a quick, comforting dinner on busier nights.*

Turkey, Stuffing & Cranberry Pot Pie

SERVES
4–6

PREP
1 hour

COOK
45 mins

Tender turkey, herby stuffing and tart cranberry all tucked under golden pastry – it's everything you love about Christmas dinner in one dish. It's brilliant made fresh but just as good thrown together with leftovers for an easy meal the following day – the perfect Boxing Day pie.

1 tbsp olive oil
600g turkey breast or thigh, cut into chunks
1 onion, finely chopped
2 carrots, diced
2 celery sticks, diced
2 garlic cloves, crushed
1 tsp dried thyme
3 tbsp plain flour
550ml chicken stock
1 tbsp wholegrain mustard
100g cranberry sauce
1 egg, beaten
1 × 325g sheet of ready-rolled puff pastry
Salt and black pepper

For the stuffing balls:
Splash of olive oil
1 onion, finely chopped
2 garlic cloves, crushed
250g sausage meat
100g fresh breadcrumbs
1 tsp dried sage
1 egg, beaten

Heat the oil in a large pan and brown the turkey pieces all over, then lift out and set aside. Add the onion, carrots and celery to the same pan and cook for 8–10 minutes until softened. Stir in the garlic and thyme, cook for another minute, then sprinkle over the flour and stir it in until everything is evenly coated. Gradually pour in the stock, stirring as you go until it thickens slightly, then stir in the mustard. Return the turkey to the pan and simmer gently for 15–20 minutes until cooked through and coated in a rich gravy. Season well and leave to cool slightly.

For the stuffing balls, preheat the oven to 220°C/200°C fan. Heat a little oil in a frying pan, add the onion and garlic and fry until soft. Combine in a bowl with the sausage meat, breadcrumbs, sage and egg, season well, then roll into small balls, transfer to a baking tray and bake for 15–20 minutes until golden.

Spoon the turkey mixture into a pie dish (approx. 30 × 25cm), scatter over the stuffing balls and dot cranberry sauce in between. Brush a little beaten egg around the rim of the dish, then lay the puff pastry over the top, pressing down the edges to seal. Brush the top with more beaten egg and cut a few small slits to let steam escape. Bake for 40–45 minutes until golden and bubbling.

- **Time-saving tip:** *This pie is ideal for using up leftovers from a Sunday roast or Christmas dinner – just mix any leftover meat, gravy, stuffing and cranberry together, top with pastry and bake until golden.*

Salmon & Dill Pie with Lemon Cream Sauce

SERVES
4–6

PREP
30 mins

COOK
45 mins

This is a brilliant midweek pie. It's quick to put together and lighter than a classic fish pie, with flaky pastry on top, tangy crème fraîche, tender salmon, sweet veg and a sauce that keeps it fresh. It's great with mash and some greens on the side.

600g salmon fillets
30g butter
1 tbsp olive oil
1 onion, finely chopped
1 carrot, finely diced
2 garlic cloves, finely chopped
1 tbsp plain flour
150ml dry white wine
250ml fish stock
200g crème fraîche
Zest and juice of 1 lemon
100g frozen peas
20g fresh dill, roughly chopped
1 × 375g sheet of ready-rolled puff pastry
1 egg, beaten
Salt and black pepper

To remove the salmon skin easily, place the fillets skin-side up on a rack set over a tray. Boil a kettle and pour the water slowly over the skin. Leave to cool, then peel it off and cut the salmon into chunks.

Melt the butter with the oil in a wide pan. Add the onion and carrot and cook gently for 8–10 minutes until softened. Stir in the garlic for another minute, then sprinkle in the flour and stir until it forms a paste. Gradually pour in the wine, whisking until smooth, then add the fish stock. Simmer for 5 minutes until slightly thickened.

Turn the heat down and stir in the crème fraîche, lemon zest and juice, then season well with salt and pepper. Add the salmon chunks and peas and cook gently for 3–4 minutes until the salmon is just beginning to turn opaque. Stir through the dill, then transfer the filling to a pie dish and leave to cool for 10 minutes.

Preheat the oven to 220°C/200°C fan. Lay the puff pastry sheet over the dish, pressing the edges against the rim. Trim the excess, cut a small hole in the centre to let the steam escape and brush with the beaten egg to glaze.

Bake for 25–30 minutes until the pastry is golden and puffed. Let it rest for 5 minutes before serving.

Beef & Stilton Pie with Rich Gravy

SERVES
6

PREP
45
mins

COOK
4¼
hours

This is all about comfort and flavour. Buttery shortcrust pastry holds tender beef that has been slow-cooked until it falls apart in a rich, glossy gravy. The gravy is deep and savoury from hours of gentle cooking and the Stilton melts through the filling to give it even more body and flavour. Together it makes for a pie that's hearty, indulgent and full of character, the kind you want to sit down to with a big pile of mash on the side.

1.5kg mix of stewing steak and beef shin
Olive oil, for frying
1 large onion, chopped
2 carrots, chopped
2 celery sticks, chopped
1 whole garlic bulb, halved horizontally
2 sprigs of rosemary
2 sprigs of thyme
2 bay leaves
2 tbsp tomato purée
150ml port
200ml red wine
750ml beef stock
250ml bone broth
1 tbsp Worcestershire sauce
80g butter
80g plain flour
100g Stilton cheese
700–800g ready-made shortcrust pastry
1 egg yolk
1 tbsp cornflour mixed with a splash of cold water
Salt and black pepper
Buttery mash, to serve

Preheat the oven to 180°C/160°C fan.

Season the beef with salt and sear in a large pan with a splash of olive oil until browned all over. Remove the meat and set aside. To the same pan, add the onion, carrots, celery, garlic, rosemary, thyme and bay leaves. Cook until softened and golden, then stir in the tomato purée.

Pour in the port and red wine and let it bubble for a couple of minutes. Add the beef stock, bone broth, Worcestershire sauce and 1 teaspoon of black pepper. Return the beef to the pan and bring to a gentle simmer. Cover and cook in the oven for 3½ hours until the beef is tender and falling apart.

Lift the meat out and shred into chunky pieces. Stir through a ladle of the braising liquid to keep it moist, then cover with foil and set aside. Increase the oven temperature to 200°C/180°C fan.

To make the filling, melt the butter in a pan, then stir in the flour to form a roux. Cook it for a minute, then gradually whisk in 250ml of the reserved braising liquid until smooth (keep the remaining liquid to make a gravy). Crumble in the Stilton and stir until melted, then fold through the shredded beef.

Roll out the pastry to a thickness of 5mm and use to line a deep pie tin. Line with baking paper and fill with baking beans, then blind bake for 15 minutes. Remove the beans and bake for another 5 minutes. Place the pastry in the fridge for 30 minutes, or in the freezer for 10–15 minutes, just to help it keep its shape. Fill the pie with the beef and Stilton mixture, top with a pastry lid, crimp the edges and decorate with any offcuts. Brush with the egg yolk and bake for 40 minutes until golden and crisp.

Strain the remaining braising liquid into a pan and reduce on the hob. Once thickened slightly, add the cornflour mixture and cook until glossy.

Serve the pie alongside buttery mash with a good glug of the gravy over the top.

● **Cost-saving tip:** *If beef shin is expensive or hard to find, use all stewing steak – it'll still break down beautifully with the long cook.*

Lamb & Rosemary Pie with Red Wine Gravy

SERVES
4–6

PREP
30
mins

COOK
2½
hours

Tender lamb slow-cooked with finely chopped rosemary, onions and carrots in a rich red wine and mint gravy, all tucked under buttery golden flaky pastry. More of a humble, home-style favourite than a showstopper, it's simple to make, especially with shop-bought pastry, and even better shared with good company.

1kg diced lamb shoulder
3 tbsp plain flour
3 tbsp olive oil
2 onions, thinly sliced
3 carrots, diced
4 garlic cloves, finely chopped
1 tbsp finely chopped fresh rosemary
2 tbsp tomato purée
400ml red wine
400ml beef stock
2 tbsp Worcestershire sauce
1 tbsp English mustard
1 tbsp mint sauce
320g ready-rolled puff pastry
1 egg, beaten
Salt and black pepper

Dust the lamb with the flour and a good crack of black pepper. Heat the olive oil in a large casserole and brown the lamb in batches until golden, setting aside on a plate once done.

Add the onions, carrots and garlic to the same casserole and cook until they are softened. Stir in the chopped rosemary and tomato purée, then pour in the red wine. Let it bubble and reduce by half before adding the stock, Worcestershire sauce, mustard and mint sauce. Return the lamb to the pan, then season with salt to taste. Cover and let it gently simmer for 1½–2 hours until the lamb is tender and the sauce has thickened into a rich gravy.

Preheat the oven to 220°C/200°C fan. Spoon the lamb filling into a deep pie dish and leave to cool slightly. Drape the pastry over the filling, pressing the edges to seal and trimming off any excess. Cut a small slit in the centre, brush with the beaten egg and bake for 35–40 minutes until golden and crisp.

Serve with your favourite veg on the side.

Bacon & Egg Pie

SERVES
6–8

PREP
25
mins

COOK
55
mins

Great for a hearty brunch with beans, a comforting lunch with slaw, or packed up cold for a picnic. Crispy bacon, sweet leeks and rich cheese, all wrapped up in buttery layers of pastry. Simple, satisfying and full of flavour.

- Butter, for greasing
- 350g ready-made shortcrust pastry
- 8 rashers of streaky bacon, chopped
- 1 large leek, trimmed, washed and thinly sliced
- 1 tbsp oil or butter
- 10 eggs, plus 1 beaten egg for brushing
- 4 tbsp double cream
- 60g mature Cheddar, grated
- 200g ready-rolled puff pastry
- Salt and black pepper

Preheat the oven to 210°C/190°C fan. Lightly grease a deep 24cm pie dish.

Roll out the shortcrust pastry to fit the dish, pressing it into the corners and up the sides and leaving a slight overhang. Prick the base lightly all over with a fork, then chill in the fridge for 20 minutes to help prevent shrinkage. Once firm, line the pastry with baking paper, fill with baking beans or rice and bake for 15 minutes. Remove the paper and beans, then return to the oven for another 5–7 minutes until the base looks dry and lightly golden. Set aside to cool slightly.

Meanwhile, fry the chopped bacon in a large frying pan over a medium heat until the fat renders and the edges start to crisp. Add the sliced leek with the oil or butter and cook gently for 5–6 minutes until softened. Season lightly and leave to cool a little.

In a bowl, whisk three of the eggs with the cream and a little salt and pepper.

Spoon half of the bacon and leek mixture into the pastry base. Crack seven whole eggs evenly over the filling, spacing them out slightly. Scatter over all the grated cheese, then spoon over the remaining bacon and leek mixture. Finally, pour over the whisked eggs and cream, letting it seep through the layers.

Brush the shortcrust pastry edge with some of the beaten egg, then lay the puff pastry sheet over the top, pressing down to seal and trimming away any excess. Crimp the edges, make a small hole or slit in the centre to let steam escape, then brush the top with the remaining beaten egg.

Bake on a tray in the centre of the oven for 45–50 minutes until the pastry is golden and crisp. Leave to rest for 10–15 minutes before slicing. This is lovely served warm with beans or slaw.

Wild Mushroom & Ale Pie with Parsnip & Thyme Mash Top

SERVES
6

PREP
30
mins

COOK
1¼
hours

Think of this as a vegetarian take on cottage pie – the mushrooms and ale give it a proper depth and heartiness, and the parsnip in the mash adds a touch of sweetness. I love it with something sharp on the side to cut through the richness, like pickled red cabbage or beetroot.

800g potatoes, peeled and cut into chunks
800g parsnips, peeled and cut into chunks
75g butter
2 egg yolks
A few sprigs of thyme, leaves picked
2 tbsp olive oil
1 onion, finely chopped
1 carrot, diced
1 celery stick, diced
3 garlic cloves, finely chopped
800g mushrooms (a mix of wild, chestnut and button), roughly chopped
300ml ale
3 tbsp plain flour
400ml vegetable stock
2 tbsp tomato purée
2 tsp soy sauce
Salt and black pepper

Get the potatoes and parsnips into a large pan of salted water, bring up to the boil and simmer until tender, around 20 minutes. Drain well, mash with the butter until smooth, then quickly beat in the egg yolks so they enrich the mash without scrambling. Stir through the thyme leaves and season with salt and pepper, then set aside.

Meanwhile, heat the olive oil in a large pan, then soften the onion, carrot and celery over a low heat for about 10 minutes. Stir in the garlic and cook for another minute. Turn the heat up, add the mushrooms and cook until golden and any liquid has evaporated. Pour in the ale and let it bubble away until nearly all the liquid has gone. Sprinkle over the flour and stir well to coat everything.

Add the stock, tomato purée and soy sauce, then simmer gently for 20–25 minutes until thickened and glossy. Taste and adjust the seasoning.

Preheat the oven to 220°C/200°C fan. Spoon the filling into a baking dish and spread the parsnip and potato mash evenly over the top, dragging a fork across to rough it up. Bake for 30 minutes until golden and crisp on top.

● **Time-saving tip:** *The filling can be made a day ahead – just cool it down, cover and refrigerate, then top with the mash and bake when you're ready.*

Chapter Five

ONE-POT WARMERS

Sausage, Apple & Cider Casserole

SERVES 4

PREP 20 mins

COOK 1 hour

Juicy sausages, sweet apples and a tangy hit of cider make this a casserole with a twist. The potatoes soak up the rich sauce while the apples soften but still keep a little bite, adding freshness. Crispy bacon on top adds a salty crunch, and with everything prepared in one pan, it's simple, hearty comfort food with a boozy kick.

---

1 tbsp olive oil
12 good-quality pork sausages
6 rashers streaky bacon, chopped
200g round shallots, peeled
5 garlic cloves, sliced
2 tbsp tomato purée
2 tbsp plain flour
500ml dry cider
300ml chicken stock
200ml water
500g Jersey Royal potatoes, halved if large
A few fresh sage leaves
Zest of 1 lemon
1 tbsp wholegrain mustard
2 tsp Worcestershire sauce
2 apples, cored and thickly sliced
Chopped chives, to finish

Preheat the oven to 200°C/180°C fan. Heat the olive oil in a large casserole pan and brown the sausages on all sides, then transfer them to a roasting tray and place them in the oven. Add the bacon to the casserole pan and cook until crisp, then remove and set aside.

Add the shallots and garlic to the pan and cook until softened. Stir through the tomato purée and flour and let it cook out for a minute before gradually pouring in the cider, stock and water, stirring well.

Tip in the potatoes, sage leaves, lemon zest, mustard and Worcestershire sauce. Return the sausages to the pan along with half the crispy bacon, then tuck in the apple slices.

Transfer to the oven and cook, uncovered, for 45 minutes until the sauce has thickened and the potatoes are tender.

Finish with the remaining bacon and a scattering of chives.

Lancashire Hotpot

SERVES
4

PREP
25
mins

COOK
1½
hours

Lancashire Hotpot has been around for centuries; a dish built on thrift and comfort. At its heart it's lamb, onions and potatoes, slow-cooked until tender. I've taken that foundation and given it a more nourishing edge with kidneys, slices of black pudding and a splash of red wine in the base. It adds a richness and depth that makes this version a little more indulgent but still every bit as warming as the one that's been enjoyed across tables in the North for generations.

500g lamb shoulder, diced
150g lamb kidneys, sliced
4 carrots, sliced
1 large onion, sliced
2 garlic cloves, finely chopped
2 tbsp flour
300ml chicken stock
200ml red wine
1 tbsp Worcestershire sauce
4 large potatoes, thinly sliced
200g black pudding, sliced
100g butter, diced
1 tsp fresh thyme leaves
Salt and black pepper

Preheat the oven to 200°C/180°C fan. Season the lamb shoulder and kidneys with salt and pepper, then brown them in a large pan until golden. Remove and set aside, then add the carrots, onion and garlic to the same pan and cook for a few minutes to soften. Sprinkle in the flour, stir to coat, then pour in the stock and wine. Add the Worcestershire sauce and bring to a simmer, then return the browned meat and cook for 20 minutes until slightly reduced.

Arrange a layer of sliced potatoes in the base of a casserole dish, then add some of the lamb mixture, then some sliced black pudding. Repeat the layers, finishing with an overlapping layer of potato on top. Dot with the butter, season well, cover with a lid or foil and bake for 1 hour. Remove the cover and cook for a further 30 minutes so the potatoes crisp up.

Scatter with the thyme leaves before serving.

Sussex Smoky with Cheddar Crust & Roasted Tenderstem Broccoli

SERVES 4

PREP 25 mins

COOK 40 mins

A hearty, comforting dish of haddock baked under a rich, cheesy sauce, sharpened with horseradish and finished with a crisp topping. Using half-smoked and half-unsmoked fish keeps the flavour balanced, while extra-mature Cheddar, Parmesan and chives bring depth. As it's a rather loose dish, it lends itself well to being baked in individual portions for serving, though a big sharing bake works just as well; it may not look quite as neat, but it tastes every bit as good.

600ml whole milk
200ml double cream
2 tsp black peppercorns
4 bay leaves
480g skin-on smoked haddock fillets
480g skin-on unsmoked haddock fillets
200g salted butter, plus optional extra for the topping
2 tbsp olive oil, plus extra for the broccoli
2 large leeks, trimmed and thinly sliced
70g plain flour
160g extra-mature Cheddar, grated
80g Parmesan, grated
4 tsp creamed horseradish
4 tbsp chives, finely chopped
240g fresh white breadcrumbs
Small handful of curly parsley, chopped
300g tenderstem broccoli
Juice of ½ lemon
Salt and black pepper

Warm the milk and cream in a wide pan with the peppercorns and bay leaves, then lay the haddock fillets in skin-side down. Bring to a gentle simmer, cover and poach for 8–10 minutes until the fish flakes easily. Lift the haddock out on to a plate and, when cool enough to handle, peel away the skin and flake the flesh into large chunks. Set aside, discarding the bay and peppercorns but keeping the poaching liquor.

Preheat the oven to 220°C/200°C fan. Melt the butter with the olive oil in another wide pan, then add the leeks with a pinch of salt and pepper and cook gently for about 8 minutes until soft. Stir in the flour to make a roux, then gradually whisk in the reserved poaching liquor until smooth and thickened. Stir through most of the Cheddar, all the Parmesan, the horseradish and most of the chives. Taste and season lightly.

Fold in the haddock and either spoon into four individual ovenproof dishes or tip into one large baking dish. Mix the breadcrumbs with the parsley and the remaining chives and Cheddar, then scatter this mix over the top. Dot with a little extra butter, if you like, and bake for 25–30 minutes until golden and bubbling.

While the fish is baking, toss the tenderstem broccoli with olive oil, lemon juice, salt and pepper. Spread it out on a baking tray and roast in the same oven for 12–15 minutes, until tender and lightly charred.

Serve the Sussex Smoky hot from the oven with the roasted broccoli on the side.

Haddock & Potato Chowder with Dill Cream & Smoked Bacon

SERVES
2

PREP
15
mins

COOK
30
mins

This is one of those bowls that delivers on richness and depth without being heavy. You've got soft chunks of potato, big flakes of smoked haddock and crispy bacon for contrast. The Dijon brings warmth, and the dill adds a fresh layer of flavour that ties everything together. Lovely with a cold, crisp glass of white wine and thick slices of crusty bread with plenty of butter.

---

1 tbsp olive oil
1 tbsp butter
150g smoked streaky bacon, finely chopped
1 small onion, finely chopped
1 celery stick, finely chopped
1 leek (white and pale green part only), thinly sliced
2 garlic cloves, finely chopped
300g floury potatoes, peeled and diced
300ml whole milk
300ml fish stock (made with 1 fish stock cube and 300ml boiling water)
2 × 200g undyed smoked haddock fillets, skin-on
1 tbsp Dijon mustard
3 tbsp double cream
1 tbsp chopped fresh dill, plus extra to garnish
Salt and black pepper
Crusty bread and butter, to serve

Heat the olive oil and butter in a large pan over a medium heat. Add the bacon and fry until golden and crispy, then scoop out a handful and set aside for the garnish. Add the onion, celery and leek to the pan and cook for 8–10 minutes, stirring occasionally, until soft. Add the garlic and cook for another minute.

Add the potatoes and stir for a few minutes, then pour in the milk and fish stock. Bring to a gentle simmer and cook for about 12 minutes, or until the potatoes are tender.

Lay the haddock fillets into the pan, skin-side down, and gently poach for 4–5 minutes until just cooked. Lift them out on to a plate and when cool enough to handle, peel off the skin and flake the flesh into large chunks.

Stir the Dijon mustard and cream into the chowder, followed by the dill. Return the haddock flakes to the pan and gently warm through. Season with black pepper and a little salt to taste.

Ladle into bowls and top with the reserved bacon and a sprinkle of dill. Serve with thick slices of crusty bread and a generous spread of butter.

Beef & Ale Cobbler with Cheese Scone Top

SERVES
4

PREP
30
mins

COOK
2½
hours

There is something really inviting about taking this out of the oven and bringing it to the table. The scones rise golden and crisp, while underneath the beef has been slowly braising in ale until it is rich and tender. Every serving brings that mix of soft stew and crunchy cheese topping, which makes it as much a showstopper as it is a comforting meal.

800g beef, diced
3 tbsp plain flour
2 tbsp olive oil
150g smoked bacon, chopped
2 large onions, sliced
3 carrots, peeled and chopped
2 celery sticks, chopped
3 garlic cloves, chopped
2 tbsp tomato purée
500ml ale
650ml beef stock
2 sprigs of thyme
2 bay leaves
1 tbsp Worcestershire sauce
Salt and black pepper

For the cheese scone topping:
250g self-raising flour
1 tsp baking powder
60g cold butter, cubed
100g mature Cheddar, grated
150ml milk
1 egg, beaten

● **Cost-saving tip:** *Beef shin or chuck works best for this dish, and they are often cheaper than ready-diced packs. Use any ale you like; there is no need for an expensive bottle, as the flavour cooks down beautifully into the gravy.*

Preheat the oven to 190°C/170°C fan. Toss the beef in the flour with a pinch of salt and pepper. Heat the oil in a large casserole pan and brown the beef in batches, transferring it to a plate as you go. Add the bacon to the same pan and fry until crisp, then add the onions, carrots, celery and garlic. Cook until softened, then stir in the tomato purée.

Pour in the ale and let it bubble for a couple of minutes, scraping the base of the pan to catch all the flavour. Add the browned beef back in with any resting juices, then pour over the stock, thyme, bay leaves and Worcestershire sauce and season with black pepper. Bring to a simmer, cover and cook in the oven for around 2 hours, or until the beef is tender.

Remove the pan from the oven and discard the thyme sprig and bay leaves. Depending on how much steam has escaped, the mixture may appear slightly dry at this stage. If so, stir in a splash of water so there is enough liquid to carry the scones as they bake uncovered.

To make the scone topping, sift the flour and baking powder into a bowl, add the butter and rub in until the mixture resembles breadcrumbs. Stir through most of the cheese, keeping a handful back for the top. Mix in the milk to form a soft dough, then roll it out on a floured surface and cut into rounds with a cutter or glass.

Arrange the scones over the beef mixture, brush them with beaten egg and scatter with the reserved cheese. Return the casserole to the oven for 20–25 minutes until the scones are golden and cooked through.

Sausage, Fennel & Butter Bean Braise with White Wine & Sage

SERVES
4

PREP
15
mins

COOK
45
mins

This dish is all about simple ingredients working together. Sausages are simmered gently with fennel, onion, sage and white wine until you have a rich, savoury broth that soaks into the butter beans. It's the sort of meal that feels just right on a chilly evening, but it's also quick and easy enough to throw together midweek when you want something hearty without too much fuss.

---

2 tbsp olive oil
12 good-quality pork sausages
1 large fennel bulb, trimmed and sliced
1 onion, thinly sliced
3 garlic cloves, finely chopped
150ml dry white wine
400ml chicken stock
3 × 400g tins butter beans, drained and rinsed
10 fresh sage leaves, chopped, plus a few extra to garnish
1 tbsp white wine vinegar
Salt and black pepper
Mash, rice or crusty bread, to serve

Heat the oil in a large casserole pan and brown the sausages until golden on all sides, then lift them out on to a plate. Add the fennel and onion to the pan and cook over a medium heat for 8–10 minutes until soft and caramelised at the edges. Stir in the garlic and cook for another minute.

Pour in the white wine, scraping up any caramelised bits from the pan, and let it bubble for 2–3 minutes to reduce slightly. Add the stock, butter beans and chopped sage, then return the sausages to the pan. Season well with black pepper and a light sprinkle of salt, if needed.

Bring to a gentle simmer, cover loosely and cook for 25–30 minutes until the sausages are cooked through and the flavours have come together. Stir in the white wine vinegar at the very end to lift the broth; then taste and adjust the seasoning.

Scatter with a few extra sage leaves before serving. Lovely served with mashed potatoes, rice or crusty bread and butter.

Lamb & Root Veg Stew with Pearl Barley

SERVES
4

PREP
25
mins

COOK
1¾
hours

Nothing fancy here, just a comforting stew. Big chunks of lamb, plenty of root veg and a bit of pearl barley to make it hearty. Great with buttery greens, or if you're really hungry, a thick slice of crusty bread and butter to mop it all up.

800g diced lamb leg, cut into 4–5cm chunks
2 tbsp plain flour
1½ tbsp vegetable oil
2 onions, roughly chopped
2 carrots, cut chunky
2 parsnips, cut chunky
200g swede, cut chunky
3 garlic cloves, crushed
1½ tbsp tomato purée
200ml red wine
800ml lamb or beef stock
2 bay leaves
100g pearl barley, rinsed
Salt and black pepper

Dust the lamb with the flour and season generously. Heat the oil in a large heavy-based casserole pan and brown the lamb in batches until well coloured, then lift out on to a plate. Add the onions, carrots, parsnips and swede to the pan and cook for 6–8 minutes until they start to catch and caramelise. Stir through the garlic and tomato purée for another minute.

Pour in the red wine and let it bubble away until reduced by half, scraping up any bits caught on the base of the pan as you go. Return the lamb to the pan with the stock and bay leaves. Bring to the boil, then lower to a gentle simmer, cover and cook for about 1 hour.

Stir in the pearl barley and cook uncovered for another 35–40 minutes until the barley is tender and the lamb is soft but still holds its shape. If the stew thickens too much, loosen with a splash of hot water or stock. Taste and adjust the seasoning before serving.

- **Cost-saving tip:** *You can use beef instead of lamb – the flavour will be slightly different but it'll still taste great.*

Ale-Braised Hunter's Chicken Stew with Bacon & Mushrooms

SERVES
4

PREP
15
mins

COOK
1½
hours

Our family lived in Tuscany for a little while when I was younger, and we'd often find ourselves at local food festivals, where bubbling pots of chicken, tomatoes and herbs filled the air. This is my take on Chicken Cacciatore, the Italian hunter's stew that's all about big flavour and rustic ingredients. I've brought that memory back home with a British twist using smoked bacon, rosemary, a bottle of ale and stock for depth. It's warming, earthy and perfect with mash or crusty bread to soak up the sauce.

---

8 bone-in, skin-on chicken thighs
2 tbsp olive oil
150g smoked streaky bacon, chopped
1 large onion, sliced
2 carrots, peeled and chopped
3 garlic cloves, finely chopped
300g chestnut mushrooms, halved
2 tbsp tomato purée
330ml amber ale
1 chicken stock cube
400g tin chopped tomatoes
1 tsp dried oregano
2 bay leaves
1 sprig of rosemary
Salt and black pepper
Buttery mash or crusty bread, to serve

Season the chicken with salt and pepper. Heat the olive oil in a large casserole pan and brown the chicken thighs in batches, starting skin-side down, until golden. Lift them out on to a plate.

Add the bacon to the pan and fry until crisp, then tip in the sliced onion and chopped carrots with a pinch of salt. Cover and cook gently for 10 minutes until soft. Stir in the garlic and cook for another couple of minutes before adding the mushrooms. Let them take on a bit of colour, then stir in the tomato purée and cook it out for a minute.

Pour in the ale and crumble in the stock cube, scraping the bottom of the pan to catch all the flavour. Add the chopped tomatoes, oregano, bay leaves and rosemary. Return the chicken to the pan, skin-side up, making sure the liquid nearly covers the meat.

Bring to a simmer, pop the lid on and cook gently for 1 hour. Take the lid off and simmer for an additional 15 minutes to allow the sauce to reduce slightly and deepen in flavour. Check the seasoning before serving.

Perfect with buttery mash or thick wedges of bread to mop up the sauce.

Pork & Mushroom Stroganoff with English Mustard & Sliced Potatoes

SERVES
2

PREP
15
mins

COOK
45
mins

This one's another staple in our family home, a no-fuss, comforting dish that always hits the spot. Pork, mushrooms and sliced potatoes cooked together in a rich mustard and paprika cream sauce – it's warm, familiar and full of flavour, the kind of meal you can count on when you want something satisfying without spending hours in the kitchen.

1 tbsp olive oil
400g pork loin, thinly sliced
1 onion, thinly sliced
2 garlic cloves, crushed
250g chestnut mushrooms, sliced
1½ tsp smoked paprika
1 tbsp plain flour
1 tbsp English mustard
100ml dry white wine
300ml chicken stock
300g waxy potatoes, thinly sliced
1 tbsp cider vinegar
150ml soured cream
Small bunch of parsley, chopped
Salt and black pepper

Heat the olive oil in a deep frying pan or shallow casserole pan over a medium heat. Season the pork with salt and pepper, then sear in batches for 2–3 minutes until golden and just cooked. Remove and set aside.

In the same pan, soften the onion for 5–6 minutes until it starts to colour. Add the garlic and cook for another minute, then throw in the mushrooms and cook until they've shrunk and taken on some colour. Stir through the paprika and flour, then add the mustard and pour in the white wine. Let it reduce for a minute, scraping the base of the pan to release all the flavour.

Add the chicken stock and bring it to a gentle simmer. Stir in the sliced potatoes, season again and add the cider vinegar. Partially cover and cook for 20–25 minutes until the potatoes are tender and the sauce has thickened.

Return the pork to the pan and let it warm through for 5 minutes. Turn off the heat, stir in the soured cream until smooth and creamy, then scatter over the chopped parsley and serve straight from the pan.

● **Cost-saving tip:** *You can swap the pork loin for pork shoulder steaks or even boneless chops to bring the cost down; just trim off any excess fat before slicing.*

Chicken Stew with Cheddar & Herb Dumplings

SERVES
4

PREP
25
mins

COOK
1¼
hours

This is the kind of dish you want when you're feeling under the weather – it's warming, filling and full of goodness. The chicken and vegetables simmer in a herby broth, while the Cheddar dumplings soak up the flavour and turn golden under the grill. It's the sort of meal that makes you feel looked after.

800g chicken breast, cut into chunks
2 tbsp plain flour
2 tbsp olive oil, plus extra as needed
1 onion, sliced
3 carrots, peeled and chopped into chunks
2 celery sticks, chopped
3 garlic cloves, finely chopped
250g chestnut mushrooms, halved
200ml dry white wine
1 tbsp Dijon mustard
800ml chicken stock
2 bay leaves
3 thyme sprigs
Salt and black pepper

For the dumplings:
50g cold butter, diced
200g self-raising flour
100g mature Cheddar, grated
2 tbsp chopped parsley
2 tbsp chopped chives
100ml whole milk

Season the chicken with salt and pepper and toss it in the flour. Heat the olive oil in a large flameproof casserole dish and sear the chicken in batches until lightly golden, lifting each batch out on to a plate once done. The flour on the chicken can soak up a fair bit of the oil, so add a little more to the pan between batches if needed to keep things frying rather than burning.

Add the onion, carrots and celery to the same pan, cooking gently until softened. Stir in the garlic and mushrooms and cook for a couple of minutes more.

Pour in the wine and let it bubble, scraping up any bits from the bottom of the pan to catch all the flavour. Stir in the mustard, return the chicken to the pan and pour over the chicken stock. Add the bay leaves and thyme sprigs, bring to a simmer, then cover and cook gently for 45 minutes until the chicken is cooked through and the vegetables are soft.

Meanwhile, make the dumplings. Rub the butter into the flour until it resembles breadcrumbs, then mix in the Cheddar and herbs. Season well with salt and pepper, then gradually add the milk, bringing the mixture together into a soft dough. Divide into 8 dumplings.

Once the stew has cooked, remove the lid and discard the thyme sprigs and bay leaves. Drop the dumplings on top of the stew, cover and simmer gently for 20 minutes until puffed. Take off the lid and place the casserole dish under a hot grill for 3–5 minutes until the dumplings are golden on top.

Hake & Chorizo One-Pot with Beans & Greens

SERVES 4

PREP 15 mins

COOK 30 mins

A quick, hearty one-pot that's packed with flavour. The smoky chorizo seasons everything it touches, the beans soak up all the juices, and the hake stays soft and flaky. It's the sort of dish you can have on the table in half an hour but still feels like something you'd order at a good pub, especially with a cold, crisp glass of white wine on the side.

- 1 tbsp olive oil, plus extra for finishing
- 200g cooking chorizo, cut into small chunks
- 1 onion, finely chopped
- 3 garlic cloves, finely chopped
- 200ml dry white wine
- 1 fish stock cube dissolved in 500ml boiling water
- 2 × 400g tins cannellini beans, drained and rinsed
- 4 hake fillets, about 150g each, skin removed
- 200g spring greens or cavolo nero, roughly shredded
- Juice of 1 lemon
- Salt and black pepper

Heat the olive oil in a large casserole pan and fry the chorizo until it releases its oils and begins to crisp. Lift it out with a slotted spoon and set aside, leaving the fat in the pan. Add the onion and cook gently until softened, then stir in the garlic. Pour in the white wine and let it bubble away until almost evaporated, then add the fish stock. Tip in the beans, season lightly and simmer for 10 minutes so the flavours develop.

Season the hake fillets and sit them on top of the beans. Cover with a lid and cook gently for 8–10 minutes until the fish flakes easily. Remove the hake, stir the greens into the hot broth to wilt, then add the hake back in and scatter with the chorizo.

Ladle into bowls and finish each plate with a drizzle of olive oil, a squeeze of lemon juice, and a pinch of salt and black pepper before serving.

● **Cost-saving tip:** *Swap the hake for cod or pollock – both work just as well and bring the price down without losing that lovely flaky texture.*

Chapter Six

THE SPECIALS BOARD

Stout Chilli con Carne

SERVES
6

PREP
25
mins

COOK
2¼
hours

Chilli con carne is a bit of a regular in our house – one of those easy-going dishes that feeds a crowd and doesn't demand too much from you but always goes down well. This version's got a little something extra. The addition of stout gives it a richer, deeper base and the bitterness of the stout cuts through the sweetness of the tomatoes and the smokiness of the spices, adding proper body and balance to the sauce. Let it simmer low and slow so all those flavours can get to know each other – and like all the best chillies, it's even better the next day.

---

2 tbsp olive oil
900g beef mince
2 onions, diced
4 garlic cloves, finely chopped
2 fresh red chillies, finely chopped
4 tbsp ground cumin
2 tbsp smoked paprika
2 tbsp ground coriander
1 tbsp chipotle paste
440ml can of stout
2 × 400g tins chopped tomatoes
2 × 400g tins kidney beans, drained
2 beef stock cubes, crumbled
1 tbsp dark soy sauce
Juice of ½ orange
Juice of 1 lime
60g fresh coriander, roughly chopped
Salt and black pepper

To serve:
Steamed rice or nachos
Pickled red onions
Grated Cheddar
Fresh chillies
Soured cream
Fresh coriander leaves

Heat the oil in a large pan over a medium heat. Add the beef mince, season with salt and pepper and cook until browned all over, breaking it up as it cooks. Once it's coloured, lift it out of the pan and set aside. Add the onions to the same pan and cook until soft, then stir in the garlic and fresh chillies. Once that's all softened and smelling good, return the browned mince to the pan.

Stir in the cumin, smoked paprika, ground coriander and chipotle paste and let that cook out for a couple of minutes. Pour in the stout to deglaze the pan, scraping up any bits from the bottom. Let it bubble for a minute or two, then add the chopped tomatoes, drained kidney beans and crumbled beef stock cubes. Bring it all to a gentle simmer and leave it bubbling away for 1 hour and 45 minutes – remove the lid halfway through cooking and make sure to give it a stir occasionally so it doesn't catch. Near the end, add the soy sauce, orange juice and lime juice and stir through the fresh coriander. Taste and adjust the seasoning with more salt and pepper if needed.

Serve with rice or nachos and top with pickled onions, grated Cheddar, fresh chillies, soured cream and more coriander.

Lamb Flatbreads with Pickled Onions, Mint Yoghurt & Pea Purée

SERVES 4

PREP 35 mins

COOK 45 mins

Warm spiced lamb on thick, pillowy flatbreads, topped with sweet pea purée, sharp pickled onions and garlicky mint yoghurt. Each bite's got richness, freshness and spice all wrapped up in your hands. It's a brilliant one for spring and summer evenings, whether you're hosting mates or just cooking something different midweek.

For the lamb:
800g lamb mince
1 large onion, finely chopped
150g mushrooms, finely chopped
4 garlic cloves, grated
1 thumb-sized piece of ginger, peeled and grated
1½ tsp ground cumin
1½ tsp ground coriander
2 tbsp tomato purée
Salt and black pepper

For the pickled onions:
200ml white wine vinegar or malt vinegar
100ml water
¾ tsp salt
6–8 black peppercorns
1 red chilli, thinly sliced
2 red onions, thinly sliced

For the flatbreads:
400g self-raising flour
400g natural yoghurt
1¼ tsp baking powder
¾ tsp salt
Fresh coriander, to garnish

Start with the pickled onions. Simmer the vinegar, water, salt, peppercorns and chilli, then pour the mixture over the sliced onions in a bowl. Leave to pickle.

Now the flatbreads: mix the flour, yoghurt, baking powder and salt into a soft dough. Knead briefly, cover and rest while you prep everything else.

For the pea purée, heat the butter and oil in a pan, add the shallot and soften for a few minutes before adding the peas and stock. Season with salt and simmer for 3–4 minutes. Use a stick blender to blitz until smooth and keep warm.

Mix the yoghurt with the fresh mint, mint sauce, garlic, lemon juice and a pinch of salt. Chill until ready to serve.

Now for the lamb. In a hot pan, brown the lamb mince. Add the onion, mushrooms, garlic and ginger and cook until soft. Stir in the cumin, coriander and tomato purée and season with salt and pepper. Let it reduce slightly and take on some colour.

Divide the dough into 4 pieces and roll each piece out into a large flatbread. Cook in a hot, dry pan for 2–3 minutes on each side until golden and puffed.

To serve, spread some pea purée over each flatbread, then top with your spiced lamb, mint yoghurt, pickled onions and a sprinkling of fresh coriander.

For the pea purée:
20g butter
2 tbsp olive oil
1 large shallot or 1 small red onion, finely chopped
500g frozen petits pois
100ml chicken or vegetable stock

For the mint yoghurt:
250g natural yoghurt
3 tbsp chopped fresh mint
1½ tsp mint sauce
1 garlic clove, grated
Juice of 1 lemon

● **Time-saving tip:** *Use good-quality shop-bought flatbreads instead. They won't be as fresh, but they'll still taste great once piled up with everything else.*

Chicken Tikka Masala with Coriander & Lime Yoghurt

SERVES
6

PREP
30
mins
(+ marinating)

COOK
1
hour

When done right, this is one of my favourite curries. Rich, creamy, spiced just enough without overpowering the charred flavour of the chicken. It's the kind of dish that makes you glad you cooked rather than ordered a takeaway. Paired with fragrant basmati rice and a zesty coriander and lime yoghurt on the side, it's everything a homemade curry should be. Bold, warming and thoroughly satisfying.

For the chicken tikka:
200g natural yoghurt
1 tbsp Kashmiri chilli powder
1 tsp ground cumin
1 tsp ground coriander
1 tsp garam masala
½ tsp ground turmeric
½ tsp ground cinnamon
½ tsp black pepper
1 tsp salt
2 tbsp tomato purée
4 garlic cloves, grated
2 tbsp grated ginger
1.2kg chicken thigh fillets

For the curry:
3 tbsp ghee
2 red onions, chopped
2 red chillies, sliced
2 tbsp grated ginger
5 garlic cloves, grated
2 tbsp tomato purée
1 tsp ground coriander
½ tsp ground cinnamon
1 tsp garam masala
1 tbsp Kashmiri chilli powder
1 tsp ground cumin
1 tsp paprika
½ tsp ground turmeric
¼ tsp ground cloves
½ tsp black pepper
¼ tsp grated nutmeg
400g tin chopped tomatoes
300ml chicken stock
2 tbsp lemon juice
1 tsp salt
1 tbsp sugar
100ml double cream

For the rice:
1 tbsp ghee
1 tsp cumin seeds
1 cinnamon stick
300g basmati rice
½ tsp ground turmeric
1 tsp salt

For the coriander and lime yoghurt:
250g full-fat Greek yoghurt
Zest and juice of ½ lime
4 tbsp finely chopped fresh coriander
½ tsp salt
¼ tsp black pepper

Start with the chicken tikka: mix the yoghurt, spices, tomato purée, garlic and ginger in a large bowl. Cut the chicken thighs into large chunks, stir them through the marinade and leave to chill for at least 2 hours or overnight if you've got the time.

Once marinated, thread the chicken pieces on to skewers and grill under a high heat or over a barbecue until they're nicely charred and just cooked through. Set aside while you make the curry.

Heat the ghee in a large deep pan and add the onions and red chillies. Cook gently for 10–15 minutes until soft and golden. Stir in the ginger and garlic and cook for a few more minutes until fragrant. Add the tomato purée and all the spices, then stir and cook for a minute to let the flavours develop.

Pour in the tinned tomatoes and chicken stock. Let it simmer for 15–20 minutes until slightly thickened. Stir in the lemon juice, salt, sugar and cream. Blend the sauce using a stick blender until smooth, then return to the heat and add the grilled chicken pieces. Let it bubble gently for 5–10 minutes so the chicken soaks up the flavour.

To make the rice, heat the ghee in a pan and toast the cumin seeds and cinnamon stick until fragrant. Stir in the rice, turmeric and salt, then pour in 600ml cold water. Bring to a simmer, cover and cook over a low heat for 10–12 minutes until the rice is tender and the water has been absorbed. Remove from the heat and let it sit for a few minutes before fluffing with a fork.

For the coriander and lime yoghurt, stir together the Greek yoghurt, lime zest and juice, chopped coriander, salt and pepper in a small bowl. Keep chilled until serving.

Spoon the curry over the rice and serve with a generous dollop of the coriander and lime yoghurt.

Mussels with Cider, Leeks, Cream & Bacon with Triple-Cooked Chips

SERVES
4

PREP
40 mins
(+ chilling)

COOK
1 hour

This one's all about a pot in the middle of the table and everyone digging in. Mussels are one of the best-value seafoods you can buy, and when you cook them with smoky bacon, sweet leeks, cider and cream, you've got a sauce that's as good as the mussels themselves. With a pile of crisp triple-cooked chips on the side, it becomes an absolute pub classic at home. If you're feeling really indulgent, you'll want some crusty bread and butter to mop up the sauce, which is quite possibly the best part!

---

2 tbsp olive oil
200g smoked streaky bacon, diced
2 leeks, trimmed and thinly sliced
2 shallots, finely chopped
3 garlic cloves, finely chopped
330ml dry cider
2kg mussels, cleaned and debearded
200ml double cream
Small bunch of parsley, chopped
Black pepper
Crusty bread and butter, to serve

For the triple-cooked chips:
700g Maris Piper potatoes
2 litres vegetable oil
Sea salt flakes

Start with the chips. Peel and cut the potatoes into thick chips, then soak them in cold water to wash off the starch. Bring a large pan of salted water to the boil and simmer the chips until just tender, about 20 minutes. Drain carefully and leave to steam-dry on a rack, then refrigerate until cold.

Heat the oil to 130°C (a digital thermometer is useful here) in a deep pan, ensuring it is no more than halfway full. Fry the chips in batches for 5 minutes until a light crust forms. Drain them on a wire rack and chill again in the fridge until completely cold.

For the mussels, heat the olive oil in a large, heavy-based pan and fry the bacon until it starts to crisp. Add the leeks and shallots and cook gently for 5 minutes until softened. Stir in the garlic and cook for an additional minute.

At this point, increase the oil temperature to 180°C and add the chips, in batches, for their final cook. Fry for 5–7 minutes until golden and crisp. Drain and season with sea salt while you finish the mussels.

Pour the cider into the bacon and leek pan and bring to the boil, then tip in the mussels, cover with a lid and cook for 5–6 minutes, shaking the pan occasionally, until the shells have opened (discard any that stay closed). Stir in the cream and let it bubble gently for a minute to bring everything together. Season with black pepper and scatter with the chopped parsley.

Serve the mussels straight from the pot, accompanied by the hot triple-cooked chips, and provide plenty of bread and butter on the table for soaking up the sauce.

Vegetable Lasagne

SERVES
6

PREP
40 mins

COOK
1 hour

You'll always spot a vegetable lasagne on pub menus as the go-to vegetarian option, but this one's so hearty you wouldn't even notice there's no meat in it. Roasting the vegetables brings out a deep flavour, the pistachios add a lovely bit of texture through the sauce and it all bakes into a bubbling, golden-topped tray that proves a veggie option can hit just as hard as the meaty ones.

- 2 yellow or red peppers, deseeded and cut into roughly 1.5cm chunks
- 1½ courgettes (about 450g), quartered lengthways and cut into roughly 1.5cm chunks
- 260g mushrooms, cut into roughly 1.5cm chunks
- 3 tbsp extra virgin olive oil
- 1½ large onions, finely chopped
- 2 carrots, diced
- 2 celery sticks, diced
- 3 garlic cloves, crushed
- 150ml red wine
- 45g shelled pistachios
- 2 × 400g tins chopped tomatoes
- ¾ tsp dried oregano
- ¾ tsp dried basil
- 1 vegetable stock cube
- 225ml cold water
- Salt and black pepper
- 10–12 dried lasagne sheets

For the cheese sauce:

- 85g butter, cubed
- 85g plain flour
- 825ml milk (whole or semi-skimmed)
- 150g mature Cheddar, grated
- 90g mozzarella, grated (or extra Cheddar)
- 45g Parmesan, grated, plus extra for topping
- Good pinch of grated nutmeg

Preheat the oven to 220°C/200°C fan. Spread the peppers, courgettes and mushrooms out on a couple of baking trays, drizzle with 2 tablespoons of the oil, season and roast for 20–25 minutes until lightly browned.

Meanwhile, heat the remaining oil in a large pan. Add the onions, carrots and celery and cook gently for 10 minutes, seasoning with salt and pepper as they soften. Stir in the garlic, then pour in the red wine and let it bubble away until reduced by half.

Lightly crush the pistachios in a pestle and mortar until they're in small, chunky pieces, then add them to the pan along with the chopped tomatoes, oregano, basil, stock cube and water. Simmer for 20 minutes – lid on for the first 10 minutes, then off for the final 10 so the sauce reduces and thickens. Stir through the roasted vegetables. Taste and adjust the seasoning.

For the cheese sauce, melt the butter in a pan and stir in the flour. Cook for 1 minute, then gradually whisk in the milk until smooth and thick. Stir in the Cheddar, mozzarella and Parmesan and season with the pinch of nutmeg and some salt and pepper.

Reduce the oven temperature to 200°C/180°C fan. Spread a thin layer of tomato sauce over the base of a large, rectangular baking dish, top with lasagne sheets, more tomato sauce, then a layer of cheese sauce. Repeat, finishing with cheese sauce and a scattering of Parmesan on top. Bake, uncovered, for 40–45 minutes until bubbling and golden, then leave to rest for 10 minutes before slicing.

Charred Chicken Caesar with Crispy Bacon & Croutons

SERVES
2

PREP
15
mins

COOK
25
mins

Quick, simple and full of flavour! This one's got juicy charred chicken, crispy bacon, golden croutons and a creamy dressing. Ideal for a midweek treat when you want something easy yet decent. And if it's the weekend, you might fancy pairing with a cold glass of white.

---

4 chicken thigh fillets, skin-on
1 garlic clove, finely grated
1 tbsp lemon juice
4 rashers of streaky bacon
2 thick slices of ciabatta, torn or cut into small chunks
1 tbsp olive oil
1 large romaine lettuce, sliced
Salt and black pepper

For the dressing:
4 anchovy fillets, finely chopped
40g finely grated Parmesan, plus extra to serve
4 tbsp Greek yoghurt
2 tbsp mayonnaise
1 tbsp Worcestershire sauce
1 tsp Dijon mustard
1 tbsp lemon juice

Season the chicken thighs with salt. Mix the grated garlic with the lemon juice and set aside.

Place the chicken skin-side down in a cold frying pan, then place over a medium-high heat. Press down with another pan or spatula for the first couple of minutes to help crisp the skin, then remove the weight and continue cooking for 7–8 minutes. While the skin side is frying, baste the top of the chicken with the lemon and garlic mix. Flip and cook for another 5 minutes, allowing the flavour to seep into the flesh side. Set aside to rest.

In the same pan, fry the bacon until crisp, then set it aside on a rack or kitchen paper.

Preheat the oven to 220°C/200°C fan. Toss the ciabatta chunks with the olive oil and some salt and pepper. Spread out on a tray and bake for 5–6 minutes until crisp and golden.

For the dressing, stir together all the ingredients and season with black pepper.

Slice the rested chicken. Toss the romaine with the dressing and pile on to plates. Top with the chicken, crispy bacon and toasted croutons. Finish with extra Parmesan, if you like.

Pork & Beef Meatballs in Tomato Sauce with Cheddar

SERVES
4

PREP
25
mins
(+ 30 mins chilling)

COOK
50
mins

My mum makes great meatballs, and this version is my take on them. Pork and beef with a touch of fennel, simmered in a rich tomato and basil sauce, then finished with sharp Cheddar melted over the top. This can be served on its own as a starter, tossed with pasta for a main, or brought to the table with crusty bread to mop up the sauce. Are they better than my mum's? No comment.

---

2 slices of white bread (with crusts)
100ml whole milk
1 tsp fennel seeds
400g pork mince
400g beef mince
1 egg
3 garlic cloves, crushed
Handful of finely chopped fresh parsley
40g grated mature Cheddar, plus extra for finishing
Olive oil, for frying
Salt and black pepper

For the sauce:
1 shallot, finely chopped
4 garlic cloves, crushed
1 red chilli, deseeded and finely chopped
A few stems of fresh basil, plus 8–10 leaves
2 tbsp tomato purée
2 × 400g tins chopped tomatoes
1 tsp sugar

Soak the bread in the milk until soft, then blend until smooth. Crush the fennel seeds in a pestle and mortar.

Add the pork and beef mince, egg and some salt and pepper to a large bowl and mix using your hands. Once combined, add the blended bread mixture, crushed garlic, parsley, Cheddar and the crushed fennel seeds. Mix until everything is evenly incorporated, then divide the mixture into 12 equal balls, weighing them if desired for consistency. Place on a tray and chill in the fridge for 30 minutes.

Heat a splash of olive oil in a large pan and brown the meatballs in batches until golden all over, then set aside while you make the sauce.

Add another splash of oil to the same pan, if needed, and gently soften the shallot. Add the garlic and chilli, then add the basil stems and leaves and cook for 1 minute until fragrant. Stir in the tomato purée and cook for another minute before adding the chopped tomatoes and sugar. Season and simmer for 20 minutes until slightly thickened. Remove and discard the basil stems and leaves.

Lower the heat and return the meatballs to the sauce. Cover and cook gently for 15–20 minutes, turning occasionally so they are evenly coated and tender all the way through.

Grate over some extra Cheddar before serving, and garnish with extra basil leaves if you like.

Worcestershire Sauce Sticky Ribs with Slaw

SERVES
4

PREP
25 mins

COOK
3 hours

I used to work as a waiter at a Tex-Mex restaurant in my hometown; they did (and still do) great BBQ ribs – slow-cooked, glazed and full of flavour. They steam-cook the ribs with fennel seeds first, which adds a subtle depth and makes the meat fall apart. These follow a similar route: cooked low and slow in cider, garlic, fennel and loads of Worcestershire sauce, then finished with a sticky glaze and a crisp slaw to cut through the richness.

---

2 tsp fennel seeds
4 garlic cloves
400ml cider
4 tbsp Worcestershire sauce
1.5kg pork spare ribs
Salt and black pepper

For the sticky glaze:
2 tbsp Worcestershire sauce
2 tbsp tomato purée
2 tbsp soft light brown sugar
1 tbsp cider vinegar
1 tbsp runny honey
1 tsp mustard powder

For the slaw:
¼ red cabbage, thinly sliced
¼ white cabbage, thinly sliced
1 large carrot, peeled and thinly sliced into matchsticks
2 tbsp mayonnaise
1 tsp Dijon mustard
Juice of ½ lemon

Preheat the oven to 180°C/160°C fan. Add the fennel seeds, garlic, cider, Worcestershire sauce and some salt and pepper to a blender and blitz for 5–10 seconds. Place the ribs in a large roasting tray, pour over the marinade and cover tightly with foil. Cook in the oven for 2½ hours – the ribs will steam gently in the liquid, becoming tender while absorbing all that flavour.

While they cook, stir together the glaze ingredients in a small pan. Bring to a simmer and reduce gently until thick and glossy.

To make the slaw, mix the red and white cabbage and carrot in a bowl. In a separate bowl, stir together the mayonnaise, Dijon mustard and lemon juice and season with salt and pepper. Toss the dressing through the veg until evenly coated.

Once the ribs are tender, take out of the oven and increase the temperature to 220°C/200°C fan. Remove the foil, baste them with the sticky glaze and return to the oven for 20–30 minutes, basting every 10 minutes until caramelised and glossy.

Serve the ribs hot as a rack or cut individually with a generous pile of crisp slaw on the side.

Thai Green Chicken Curry with Leeks & Garden Peas

SERVES
4

PREP
15
mins

COOK
30
mins

This one takes me back to Thailand when I was twenty-one, travelling with my brother and a few mates. We lived off green curry and som tam salad, and it saw us through long bus/train rides, cheap hotels, and plenty of Chang-overs. It was inexpensive, comforting and full of flavour. This version retains the same bold taste, but I've added leeks and peas for a touch of home comfort.

---

2 tbsp vegetable oil
3 tbsp Thai green curry paste
1 thumb-sized piece of ginger, peeled and roughly chopped, plus a few matchsticks to garnish
3 garlic cloves, roughly chopped
2 stalks of lemongrass, bashed
2 whole bird's eye chillies, plus a few chilli slices to garnish
4 kaffir lime leaves
400ml tin coconut milk
250ml chicken stock
Juice of 1 lime
1 tbsp fish sauce
2½ tbsp sugar
500g chicken breast, thinly sliced
2 leeks, halved and thinly sliced
150g frozen peas
Small handful of coriander leaves, plus extra to garnish
Steamed jasmine rice, to serve

Start by heating the oil in a pan over a medium heat. Add the curry paste and fry for 2 minutes, stirring constantly to prevent burning, until it darkens slightly and smells intense and fragrant.

Throw in the ginger, garlic, bashed lemongrass, whole chillies and lime leaves. Cook for another 2–3 minutes until everything softens and releases its oils.

Pour in the coconut milk and let it bubble gently for about 5 minutes until the oil starts to split and rise to the top.

Add the chicken stock, lime juice, fish sauce and sugar. Stir well and bring it back to a gentle simmer. Once it's bubbling, add the chopped chicken and stir it through.

Let the chicken poach gently for 8–10 minutes, or until cooked through. Stir in the leeks and peas and cook for an additional minute or two – the leeks should soften but still retain a bit of bite.

Stir through a handful of coriander just before serving. Serve spooned over steamed jasmine rice and scatter with ginger matchsticks, sliced chillies and a few more coriander leaves.

Beetroot Crumble Bake with Goat's Cheese Custard

SERVES
6

PREP
25
mins

COOK
1¼
hours

Sweet, earthy beetroot baked under a nutty, savoury crumble, with a warm goat's cheese custard poured over at the table. It's the sort of dish that sits somewhere between comforting and elegant, ideal for a Sunday-lunch centrepiece or a simple supper with a glass of white wine.

900g raw beetroot, peeled and cut into wedges
1 large red onion, sliced
2 garlic cloves, finely chopped
3 tbsp olive oil
1½ tbsp balsamic vinegar
1½ tsp thyme leaves
Salt and black pepper

For the crumble:
135g cold butter, cubed
190g plain flour
75g rolled oats
25g panko breadcrumbs
50g grated Parmesan
30g grated mature Cheddar
75g chopped walnuts

For the goat's cheese custard:
225ml double cream
150ml whole milk
3 egg yolks
125g soft goat's cheese
1 tsp Dijon mustard

Preheat the oven to 210°C/190°C fan. Add the beetroot, red onion and garlic to a large baking dish and toss with the olive oil, balsamic vinegar, thyme leaves and some salt and pepper so everything's well coated. Cover with foil and roast for 20 minutes to start softening the beetroot, then remove the foil and roast uncovered for another 25–30 minutes, stirring halfway, until tender and lightly caramelised around the edges. If there's too much liquid in the dish, spoon a little out before you add the topping so the crumble stays crisp.

Meanwhile, make the crumble. Rub the butter into the flour with your fingertips until it forms rough breadcrumbs, then stir in the oats, panko, Parmesan, Cheddar and walnuts. Mix thoroughly so the cheese is evenly spread through the mixture – you want small clumps rather than a dry mix.

Once the beetroot is cooked, spoon the crumble mixture evenly over the top and bake for 30 minutes until golden and crisp, with the cheese melted through and the nuts lightly toasted.

While the crumble is in the oven, make the goat's cheese custard. Gently heat the cream and milk in a pan until just steaming. Whisk the egg yolks in a bowl, then slowly pour the warm liquid into the bowl, whisking constantly. Return the mixture to the pan over a low heat and stir until it thickens slightly and coats the back of a spoon – don't let it boil. Remove from the heat, crumble in the goat's cheese and add the Dijon mustard. Season to taste with salt and pepper, whisking until smooth.

Spoon generous portions of the beetroot bake on to plates and serve with the warm goat's cheese custard poured over the top.

Ozs.
10

Chapter Seven

NOT JUST ANY POTATOES

Hasselback Potatoes with Cheddar & Herb Crumb

SERVES
4

PREP
20
mins

COOK
1
hour

These potatoes were a viral sensation on social media, and this is my version. Crisp slices roast until golden with buttery centres, the Cheddar melting into every cut, while a golden, vibrant crumb of bread, herbs and lemon zest brings freshness and crunch. They're the sort of side that lifts anything you put them next to, perfect with meat and fish.

---

12 small-medium Maris Piper potatoes
50g butter
6 tbsp olive oil
4 garlic cloves, crushed
1½ slices of white bread
10g fresh parsley
10g fresh chives
Zest of 1 lemon
60g mature Cheddar, finely grated
Salt and black pepper

Preheat the oven to 200°C/180°C fan. Slice each potato three-quarters of the way down at 5mm intervals. Positioning them between two wooden spoons helps stop you from cutting all the way through.

Melt the butter with 4 tablespoons of the olive oil and the garlic in a small pan over a low heat for 5 minutes to infuse, then take it off the heat.

Place the potatoes in a roasting tray, cut sides up. Spoon the garlic butter and oil over the potatoes, ensuring it runs between the cuts, then, season generously with salt and pepper. Roast for 50–60 minutes, basting halfway through.

Tear the bread into coarse crumbs and blitz in a food processor with the parsley, chives and lemon zest until a coarse texture forms. Heat the remaining 2 tablespoons of olive oil in a frying pan over a medium heat. Add the crumb mixture and fry, stirring, until crisp and golden, then season with a pinch of salt.

Remove the tray of potatoes 10–15 minutes before the end of the cooking time and scatter the grated Cheddar over them, then return to the oven to melt. Finish with the golden, vibrant crumb just before serving.

Herby Dauphinoise with Mustard Cream

SERVES
6–8

PREP
25
mins

COOK
1 hr 20
mins

The first time I tried dauphinoise was in the South of France. I'd ordered a steak, but to be honest, I don't really remember the meat – it was the potatoes that stole the show. Silky layers melting together with cream, garlic and herbs, bubbling away until the top was golden. My take features English mustard for a little kick, Cheddar for richness and rosemary and thyme to elevate it all. You get that mix of soft, tender potatoes underneath with a crisp, cheesy crust on top – a side dish that's all about flavour and texture.

2kg Maris Piper potatoes
600ml double cream
400ml whole milk
3 garlic cloves, thinly sliced
3 sprigs of fresh rosemary
4 sprigs of fresh thyme
2 tsp English mustard
80g butter
140g mature Cheddar, grated
40g Parmesan, finely grated
Salt and black pepper

Time-saving tip: *You can bake the dish to the first stage (covered with foil), then cool and keep it covered in the fridge. When ready to serve, finish it at 220°C/200°C fan until golden and piping hot – perfect for getting ahead before guests arrive.*

Peel the potatoes and slice them 3–4mm thick, using a mandoline if you have one. Drop the slices into a large bowl of cold water as you go to wash off some of the starch, then drain and pat dry with a clean tea towel.

In a pan, warm the cream and milk with the garlic and rosemary and thyme sprigs. Let it gently heat until just below a simmer, then remove from the heat and let it infuse for 10 minutes. Strain out the herbs, stir in the mustard and season well with salt and pepper. Keep the cream mixture warm.

Preheat the oven to 200°C/180°C fan.

Rub the inside of a large deep baking dish with a bit of the butter, then start layering the potatoes, overlapping them slightly. After the first couple of layers, ladle over some of the cream mix and scatter with Cheddar. Continue building up the layers until everything is used up. Finish with cream and a final scattering of Cheddar and Parmesan. Dot the top with the remaining butter.

Cover with foil and bake for 40–50 minutes. Remove the foil, increase the oven temperature to 220°C/200°C fan and bake for a further 20–30 minutes until the top is golden, bubbling and crisp around the edges. Depending on the depth of your dish, the timing can shift slightly – shallower trays will cook faster, while deeper ones require longer cooking times.

Leave it to sit for 10 minutes before serving so the layers hold together nicely when sliced.

The Ultimate Roast Potatoes with Garlic & Rosemary

SERVES
6

PREP
15
mins

COOK
1 hr 10
mins

We can all agree that the star of a Sunday roast is the roast potatoes. Get these right and you'll be crowned king or queen of the table. Fluffy inside, golden and crisp on the outside, these are cooked first with garlic, rosemary and beef stock for extra flavour, then finished in plenty of duck fat with more garlic and rosemary at the end. These are the roasties everyone fights over.

1.5kg Maris Piper potatoes
2 beef stock cubes
6 garlic cloves, 4 bashed and 2 finely chopped
4 sprigs of rosemary
2 sprigs of thyme
300g duck fat (or olive oil)
1 tbsp olive oil
Sea salt flakes

Time-saving tip: *Roast the potatoes in the morning before everything else goes in the oven. Once cooked, leave them uncovered to prevent them from steaming and becoming soft. Keep them out of reach of the family; otherwise, you'll find they've disappeared before lunch is served. Reheat them in an oven preheated to 220°C/200°C fan for 10 minutes.*

Peel and cut the potatoes into large, even chunks. Put them into a large pan with about 2 litres cold water, the beef stock cubes, bashed garlic cloves, 2 of the rosemary sprigs, the thyme sprigs and a good pinch of salt. Bring to a simmer and gently poach for 10–15 minutes until just tender.

Lift the potatoes carefully out with a slotted spoon on to a wire rack to air-dry – this helps the edges rough up, which is what gives you that crisp finish.

Preheat the oven to 220°C/200°C fan. Place the duck fat (or olive oil) in a large roasting tray and put it in the oven until it's smoking hot.

Tip the potatoes into the tray and very carefully spoon the hot fat over them. Avoid moving them around too much at this stage, so you keep those rough edges intact. Roast for 30 minutes, then turn gently. Continue roasting for another 25–30 minutes, turning a couple of times as they cook, so they colour evenly and develop a proper crunch.

About 10 minutes before the potatoes are ready, strip the rosemary leaves from the remaining sprigs and chop finely, then mix with the 2 finely chopped garlic cloves and tablespoon of olive oil and scatter over the potatoes. Return to the oven until intensely aromatic.

Remove from the tray and finish with a generous sprinkling of sea salt flakes before serving.

Cheddar & Truffle Mash with Black Pepper & Butter

SERVES
4

PREP
15
mins

COOK
1 hr 20
mins

This isn't your everyday mash; it's rich, cheesy and packed with flavour. The Cheddar lends it boldness, the truffle adds an earthy depth, and the black pepper keeps it lively. It's the kind of mash that makes the meat almost feel like an extra, and it pairs really well with roast chicken, a good cut of beef, or pork chops, plus some greens on the side.

1.5kg Maris Piper potatoes
75g butter, melted
150g extra-mature Cheddar, grated
1 tbsp truffle oil (or to taste)
1 tsp cracked black pepper
Olive oil
Salt
Freshly grated truffle (optional)

- **Cost-saving tip:** *If truffle oil is hard to find or out of budget, leave it out – you'll still have a cracking Cheddar mash that's full of flavour.*

- **Time-saving tip:** *You can boil the potatoes instead of baking them, but they'll hold more moisture so the mash won't be quite as fluffy or intense.*

Preheat the oven to 220C°C/200°C fan. Prick the potatoes all over with a fork, then bake them whole for about an hour until the skins are crisp and the insides soft. Remove the potatoes from the oven, cut them in half and scoop the flesh into a bowl. Pass it through a potato ricer or mash until smooth. Pour in the melted butter, then immediately stir through the Cheddar so it melts evenly into the mash. Add the truffle oil and cracked black pepper, mixing until the sauce is rich and creamy.

Flatten the empty potato skins on a baking tray, drizzle with olive oil and season with salt and pepper. Return to the oven for 15–20 minutes until crisp – they make a perfect crunchy extra on the side.

For an extra flourish, you can finish the mash with a little freshly grated truffle on top.

Roast Spicy Bombay Potatoes with Coriander & Lime Yoghurt

SERVES
4

PREP
15
mins

COOK
1
hour

Crispy spuds are always a winner, but give them a kick of chilli, cumin and mustard seeds and you're on to something special. I love putting a plate piled high of these down in the middle of the table; they're hot, spicy, sharp from the yoghurt, and nothing goes better with them than an ice-cold lager. Cracking food for sharing with mates or sticking next to a curry.

1kg baby potatoes, halved
3 tbsp vegetable oil
1 tsp mustard seeds
1 tsp cumin seeds
1 onion, thinly sliced
5 garlic cloves, finely chopped
1 red chilli, finely chopped
1 tsp ground cumin
1 tsp ground coriander
1 tsp ground turmeric
1 tsp paprika
1 tsp garam masala
1 tbsp tomato purée
Small bunch of coriander, chopped
Salt and black pepper

For the yoghurt:
200g natural yoghurt
Juice of 1 lime
1 tsp ground cumin
Small bunch of coriander, finely chopped

Preheat the oven to 220°C/200°C fan. Boil the potatoes in salted water for 8–10 minutes until just tender. then drain and steam-dry. Spread them out on a baking tray, drizzle with 2 tablespoons of the vegetable oil and season generously with salt. Roast for 45–50 minutes, turning halfway through, until crisp and golden.

Meanwhile, heat the remaining oil in a large frying pan. Add the mustard seeds and cumin seeds and let them pop, then stir in the onion. Cook gently until softened and golden, then add the garlic and red chilli. Stir in the ground spices, cooking for 1 minute until fragrant, then add the tomato purée and about 100–150ml water to loosen into a thick sauce.

Tip the roasted potatoes into the pan and toss well so they're coated in the spiced onion mixture. Stir through the chopped coriander and season to taste.

Mix the yoghurt with the lime juice, ground cumin and chopped coriander and season with salt and pepper. Serve the potatoes hot with a dollop of the coriander and lime yoghurt on the side.

Smashed Potatoes with Garlic Butter & Parmesan Crust

SERVES
4

PREP
15
mins

COOK
50
mins

Golden, crisp on the outside and soft in the middle, these smashed potatoes always deliver. With plenty of crunch, the richness of garlic butter and that salty hit of Parmesan, they make a brilliant option for steak night or when you want something a little bit extra midweek.

1.2kg baby potatoes
4 tbsp olive oil
100g butter, melted
4 garlic cloves, finely grated
60g Parmesan, finely grated
1 tbsp chopped fresh parsley
Black pepper

Boil the potatoes in a large pan of salted water until tender, about 20–25 minutes. Drain and steam-dry for a couple of minutes, then tip them on to a large baking tray lined with baking paper. Use the base of a glass or a potato masher to gently press each one down until flattened but still holding together. Drizzle with the olive oil and season with black pepper.

Preheat the oven to 220°C/200°C fan.

Mix the melted butter with the garlic, then spoon it generously over the smashed potatoes. Scatter with the Parmesan and roast for 25 minutes until golden, crisp and bubbling at the edges. Finish with the chopped parsley before serving.

Roasted Beef Dripping & Thyme Chips

SERVES
4

PREP
15
mins

COOK
55
mins

These are chips taken to the next level. Boiled in stock with garlic and thyme so the flavour goes right to the core, then roasted in beef dripping until golden, crisp and fluffy inside. They've got that deep, comforting Sunday roast flavour and are perfect on their own, as a side to meat or just with a jug of gravy.

1.2kg Maris Piper potatoes
2 beef stock cubes
8 sprigs of thyme
4 garlic cloves, bashed
100g beef dripping
Salt

Peel the potatoes and cut them into thick chip-like batons. Place them in a large pan of cold water along with the stock cubes, 4 of the thyme sprigs and the garlic cloves. Bring to the boil and simmer for 6–7 minutes until just tender but not falling apart. Drain well, discard the thyme and garlic, and leave on a wire rack to steam-dry.

Preheat the oven to 220°C/200°C fan. Place the beef dripping in a large roasting tray and put into the oven until it's smoking hot. Carefully tip in the potatoes, ensuring they're evenly coated, and season with salt. Roast for 30 minutes, then turn them over and continue roasting for another 15 minutes. Scatter the leaves from the remaining 4 thyme sprigs over the top and roast for a final 10 minutes until the chips are golden and crisp.

Serve straight from the tray with more salt if needed.

Time-saving tip: *You can parboil the potatoes earlier in the day, drain and leave them uncovered at room temperature. When it's nearly time to eat, roast them in the hot dripping so they come out perfectly crisp without losing any crunch.*

Rosemary & Sea Salt Chips with Malt Vinegar Dust

SERVES
4

PREP
30
mins
(+ chilling)

COOK
40
mins

Classic chippy flavours lifted with aromatic rosemary and a tangy malt vinegar dust that gives the chips a sharp, savoury edge and loads of flavour.

700g Maris Piper potatoes
2 sprigs of rosemary leaves, very finely chopped
Vegetable oil, for deep-frying (about 2 litres)
Malt vinegar
Sea salt flakes

Peel and cut the potatoes into thick chips, then soak them in cold water for 10 minutes to wash off the starch.

Bring a large pan of salted water to the boil with a half the rosemary sprigs. Simmer the chips until just tender, about 8–10 minutes, then drain carefully and leave to steam-dry on a wire rack. Once cool, refrigerate until completely cold.

Half-fill a deep pan with vegetable oil and heat to 130°C. Fry the chips in batches for about 5 minutes, just until a light crust forms. Drain on a rack and chill again in the fridge until fully cold.

Meanwhile, make the malt vinegar dust. Pour a thin layer of malt vinegar into a small non-stick pan, add a good pinch of sea salt, and simmer gently until all the liquid has evaporated and fine salt crystals start to form. Scrape these into a pestle and mortar and grind to a fine powder.

When ready to eat, reheat the oil to 180°C and fry the chips in batches until golden and crisp. Drain well, then toss with the remaining chopped rosemary and the malt vinegar dust while still hot.

Chapter Eight

ANY SIDES WITH THAT?

Cauliflower Cheese with Cheddar, Ale Sauce & Crispy Crumb

SERVES
6

PREP
20
mins

COOK
50
mins

This has to be one of my favourite parts of a roast dinner: roasted cauliflower covered in a rich Cheddar and ale sauce, plenty of melted cheese and a golden crumb. I love it when it's bubbling fresh from the oven, but I'll happily eat it cold the next day straight out of the tray. It's indulgent, comforting and makes a cracking addition to Christmas dinner.

---

1 large cauliflower, cut into florets, stalk and leaves chopped
2 tbsp olive oil
75g butter
75g plain flour
250ml real ale
400ml whole milk
250g mature Cheddar, grated
1 tsp Dijon mustard
½ tsp grated nutmeg (optional)
50g Gruyère, grated
50g Parmesan, grated
50g panko breadcrumbs
Salt and black pepper

Preheat the oven to 220°C/200°C fan. Place the cauliflower florets, chopped stalk and leaves on a baking tray, drizzle with the olive oil and season with salt and pepper. Toss well, then roast for 20–25 minutes, turning halfway, until golden and slightly charred on the outside.

Meanwhile, melt the butter in a pan over a low heat, then whisk in the flour and cook for 2–3 minutes to eliminate the raw flour taste. Gradually whisk in the ale, then the milk, until you have a smooth sauce. Let it bubble until thickened, then stir in 150g of the Cheddar until melted through. Add the mustard and nutmeg (if using) and season well with salt and pepper.

Tip the roasted cauliflower into a large ovenproof dish and pour the sauce over the top, making sure everything is well coated. Scatter the cheeses in layers – the remaining Cheddar first, then the Gruyère, then the Parmesan – and finish with the panko and a sprinkle of black pepper.

Bake for 20–25 minutes until golden, bubbling and crisp on top. Leave to stand for a few minutes before serving.

Never-Fail Yorkshire Puddings

MAKES
12

PREP
10
mins
(+ 30 mins resting)

COOK
20–25
mins

For me, a roast isn't complete without Yorkshire puddings – they carry the gravy, prop up the roast and make the whole plate come together. Half the joy is seeing what weird and wonderful shapes they puff into in the oven. Follow these steps and you'll get guaranteed golden results – just whatever you do, don't open the door too early, or you'll be left with Yorkshire pancakes.

---

3 eggs
250ml whole milk
110g plain flour
1 tsp salt
1 tsp white pepper
6 tbsp beef dripping

Crack the eggs into a jug with the milk and whisk until smooth. Add the flour, salt and pepper to a mixing bowl, then slowly whisk in the egg and milk mixture until the batter is lump-free. It should be the consistency of single cream; if it's too thick, add a splash more milk. Rest the batter for at least 30 minutes at room temperature, or chill in the fridge overnight if you prefer to get ahead. Just remember to bring it back to room temperature before baking, as cold batter won't rise as well.

Preheat the oven to 240°C/220°C fan. Place a 12-hole muffin tin on a baking tray and drop about half a tablespoon of beef dripping into each hole. Put it in the oven for 8–10 minutes until the fat is properly smoking hot. You'll see a faint haze and smell it. To be sure, drop in a tiny bit of batter; if it spits instantly, you're ready to go.

Working quickly, pour the batter into the tin so each hole is just under half-full. Slide it straight back into the oven and bake for 20–25 minutes until the puddings are tall, golden and crisp. Resist the urge to open the oven door while they're baking; you'll let the heat escape and ruin the rise. They're at their very best served straight from the oven while puffed up and crunchy. If you need to get ahead, though, you can bake them earlier in the day, let them cool, and then reheat in a hot oven for a few minutes before serving; they'll still come back crisp.

Smashed Sprouts with Bacon

SERVES 4

PREP 15 mins

COOK 40 mins

This is one of those sides that can convert even the sprout haters. Boiled until just tender, smashed flat, then roasted until crisp around the edges, they're finished with salty bacon and a splash of balsamic that takes away some of the bitterness. Simple, tasty and a great way to show off sprouts.

600g Brussels sprouts, trimmed
3 tbsp olive oil
2 tbsp balsamic vinegar
6 rashers of smoked streaky bacon, chopped
Salt and black pepper

Preheat the oven to 220°C/200°C fan.

Bring a large pan of salted water to the boil and cook the sprouts for 8–10 minutes, or until just tender. Drain them well, then spread them out on a large baking tray. Using the base of a glass or a potato masher, gently press each sprout until it is flattened but still holds together. Drizzle with the olive oil and season with plenty of black pepper. Roast in the oven for 20–25 minutes.

Ten minutes before the end of the cooking time, drizzle the balsamic over the sprouts and return to the oven. Meanwhile, fry the bacon in a pan until crisp. Once the sprouts are ready, toss them with the bacon and transfer to a serving plate.

Braised Red Cabbage with Apple

SERVES
8–10

PREP
15
mins

COOK
45
mins

A proper winter side – sweet, tangy and gently spiced. The apples melt down into the cabbage, giving it a lovely balance of sharp and sweet. It's great alongside pork, duck, or anything roasted.

15g butter, plus extra to finish
1 tbsp olive oil
1 large onion, thinly sliced
1 garlic clove, finely chopped
¼ whole nutmeg, freshly grated
1kg red cabbage, thinly sliced
3 tbsp light brown sugar
450g cooking apples, peeled, cored and chopped
3 tbsp red wine vinegar
Salt and black pepper

Melt the butter with the oil in a large pan over a medium heat. Add the onion and cook gently until soft and translucent. Stir through the garlic and nutmeg, then tip in the cabbage and toss for a few minutes until it starts to glisten and soften slightly.

Add the sugar, apples and vinegar, season with salt and pepper, then cover the pan with a lid. Let it cook over a low heat for about 30 minutes, giving it a stir now and again so nothing catches on the bottom.

Remove the lid and cook for another 10 minutes until everything is soft, glossy and slightly sticky. Finish with a large knob of butter, stir it through to melt and serve warm.

Photo overleaf, clockwise from top left: *Buttered Greens with Crispy Shallots (page 184), Never-Fail Yorkshire Puddings (page 179), Braised Red Cabbage with Apple, Smashed Sprouts with Bacon, Cheesy Leeks (page 185), Sticky Honey Carrots (page 178).*

Buttered Greens with Crispy Shallots

SERVES
4

PREP
10
mins

COOK
15
mins

Simple, buttery and full of flavour – these greens are lifted with garlic and topped with sweet, crunchy shallots. Perfect alongside a roast, steak, or anything rich that needs a bit of freshness.

---

1 tbsp plain flour
1 tbsp cornflour
2 large shallots, very thinly sliced lengthways
Vegetable oil, for frying
450g spring greens, trimmed and sliced
450g cavolo nero, stalks removed and sliced
40g butter
4 garlic cloves, very finely chopped
Salt

Start with the shallots so they keep their crunch. Mix the plain flour and cornflour together, then toss the sliced shallots through until evenly coated. Heat a layer of vegetable oil in a frying pan over a medium-high heat and fry the shallots in small batches until golden and crisp. Lift out on to kitchen paper and season lightly with salt.

Bring a large pan of salted water to the boil and cook the spring greens and cavolo nero for 3–4 minutes until tender but still bright. Drain well. In a separate pan, melt the butter over a medium heat, add the garlic and cook gently until fragrant. Toss the hot greens through the garlic butter until glossy and coated.

Pile the buttery greens on to a warm serving dish and finish with a generous scattering of crispy shallots on top.

Cheesy Leeks

SERVES
4

PREP
15
mins

COOK
30
mins

Tender leeks in a creamy, tangy cheese sauce, topped with bubbling Cheddar, this is a simple side that punches above its weight. Standing the leeks upright in the dish makes it look neat and presentable, and by keeping them in chunky pieces, you still get that lovely bite of leek rather than it all disappearing into the sauce. Works brilliantly next to roast chicken or pork, or even with bangers and mash for something a bit different.

---

4 large leeks
35g butter, plus extra for the dish
35g plain flour
420ml whole milk
2 tsp Dijon mustard
160g mature Cheddar, grated
Salt and black pepper

Preheat the oven to 220°C/200°C fan.

Trim the root and dark green ends from the leeks, then slice them into chunky cylinders, about 5–6cm long. Rinse carefully under cold water to remove any grit from inside the layers, then pat them dry with kitchen paper.

Heat a dry frying pan and sear the leeks, cut-sides down, until golden. Then, sear the sides. Gently roll them to get some colour around the edges – you're just looking for a bit of char to boost the flavour.

Melt the butter in a pan over a medium heat. Stir in the flour and cook for 1 minute, then gradually whisk in the milk until smooth and thickened. Remove from the heat, stir in the Dijon and 120g of the Cheddar, and season with a pinch of salt and some black pepper.

Butter a baking dish and stand the leeks upright, packed snugly. Pour the cheese sauce over the top, letting it run into all the gaps. Sprinkle the remaining 40g of Cheddar over the top and bake for 15–20 minutes until golden and bubbling.

Brown Sauce

SERVES 8

PREP 15 mins

COOK 1 hour

My favourite breakfast sandwich accompaniment – rich, tangy, fruity and just the right amount of spice. Perfect with bacon, eggs and sausage.

Splash of vegetable oil
1 white onion, finely chopped
2 garlic cloves, chopped
115g prunes, chopped
115g dates, chopped
2 Granny Smith apples, diced
190g dark brown sugar
15g salt
425ml malt vinegar
½ tsp ground ginger
¼ tsp ground allspice
¼ tsp cayenne pepper
¼ tsp grated nutmeg
1 tsp black treacle
2 tbsp soy sauce

Heat a little oil in a saucepan and fry the onion and garlic until softened. Add the remaining ingredients and bring to a gentle simmer. Cook for 45–60 minutes, stirring occasionally, until thickened and the fruit has broken down.

Blend until smooth with a stick blender, then pass through a fine sieve if you'd like it really smooth. Return to the pan and simmer a little longer if you'd like it thicker, then leave to cool before bottling. Store in the fridge for 3–4 weeks.

Hot English Mustard Mayo

SERVES 4

PREP 5 mins

A fiery, tangy little number that brings heat, depth and a good kick of mustard – perfect for burgers, grilled chicken or even chips.

3 tbsp mayonnaise
1 tsp English mustard
1 tsp wholegrain mustard
1 tbsp Worcestershire sauce
1 tsp Tabasco

Mix all the ingredients in a small bowl until smooth. Taste and tweak the heat to your liking. This will keep in the fridge for a few days in a sealed container.

British Green Sauce

SERVES
4–6

PREP
15
mins

A lively, tangy sauce made with parsley, mint, capers and anchovies, lifted with English mustard and cider vinegar. It's bright, herby and sharp – brilliant with lamb, fish or spooned over hot new potatoes.

50g flat-leaf parsley, roughly chopped
20g mint leaves, picked
4 anchovy fillets
2 tbsp capers, drained
1 small garlic clove
1 tbsp English mustard
2 tbsp cider vinegar
150ml extra virgin olive oil
Black pepper

Put the parsley, mint, anchovies, capers and garlic into a food processor and pulse until finely chopped. Add the mustard and vinegar, then slowly pour in the olive oil while blending until it comes together into a loose, spoonable sauce. Taste and season with black pepper – you won't need salt as the anchovies and capers already bring plenty.

Best made fresh, but it'll keep covered in the fridge for up to 2 days.

Sticky Sandwich Pickle

SERVES
4

PREP
10
mins

COOK
15–20
mins

You can't beat a good pickle, and this one's got everything – tang, sweetness, spice and a bit of crunch. Perfect with cheese, pork pie, or piled into a sandwich after a long walk.

---

2 carrots, peeled and diced
1 red onion, diced
1 apple, diced
100ml cider vinegar
1 tbsp golden granulated sugar
1 tbsp dark muscovado sugar
1 tsp ground allspice
1 tbsp Dijon mustard

Add all the ingredients to a pan, bring to a gentle simmer and cook for 15–20 minutes, stirring occasionally, until thickened but still with a bit of bite. Leave to cool slightly, then pulse with a stick blender just enough to smooth it out a little while keeping some texture.

- **Time-saving tip:** *You can make this pickle ahead and keep it in a clean, sterilised jar in the fridge for up to 2 weeks – the flavour only gets better.*

Apple & Wholegrain Mustard Slaw

SERVES
4–6

PREP
20
mins

Sweet, sharp and crunchy, this slaw brings a lovely balance of flavours – crisp apple, peppery mustard and tangy dressing. It's a simple one to throw together and goes perfectly with roast pork, burgers or anything off the barbecue.

150g mayonnaise
2 tbsp wholegrain mustard
1 tbsp cider vinegar
1 tsp honey
300g red cabbage, finely shredded
2 carrots, peeled and grated
2 eating apples, cored and thinly sliced into matchsticks
1 small red onion, thinly sliced

In a large bowl, whisk together the mayonnaise, wholegrain mustard, cider vinegar and honey until smooth. Taste and adjust if you'd like it sharper or sweeter.

Add the red cabbage, carrots, apples and onion, then toss everything well so that the dressing coats all the vegetables. Leave for at least 15 minutes before serving so the flavours come together.

Beer & Bacon Jam

SERVES
4–6

PREP
10
mins

COOK
1 hr 10
mins

Sweet, smoky and rich with ale and treacle, this jam's the ultimate pub-style condiment – brilliant on burgers, cheese on toast or anything that needs a hit of savoury sweetness.

225g smoked bacon
3 tbsp butter
5 large red onions, finely diced
5 garlic cloves, finely chopped
½ tsp dried thyme
1 tsp freshly ground black pepper
225ml ale
60ml golden syrup
60ml dark treacle
60ml balsamic vinegar

Fry the bacon in a large pan, without fat, over a medium heat until crisp and golden. Remove it from the pan and roughly chop into small pieces, leaving a few tablespoons of the rendered fat behind. Add the butter and onions to the pan and cook slowly for about 20–25 minutes, stirring often, until soft, sweet and starting to caramelise.

Add the garlic, thyme and black pepper and cook for another couple of minutes, then pour in the ale, scraping up all the flavour from the bottom of the pan. Let it simmer until reduced by half.

Stir in the golden syrup, dark treacle and balsamic vinegar and then the chopped bacon. Reduce the heat to low and simmer gently for around 30 minutes, stirring now and again, until thick, glossy and jammy.

Let it cool slightly before spooning into clean, sterilised jars. Store in the fridge for up to 2 weeks.

Chapter Nine

PERFECT PUDDINGS

Rhubarb Crumble with Orange Crème Fraîche

SERVES
4

PREP
15
mins

COOK
40–45
mins

This one brings back memories of the house I lived in as a child. In our garden, we had a big old rhubarb patch. When it was in season (late March to June), my parents would always make rhubarb crumble with custard – warm, sweet and sharp all at once. This is my version, featuring a thick crumble topping with a few nuts in the mix to add that extra bit of texture, served with a fresh, cool and zesty crème fraîche.

600g rhubarb, chopped
Butter, for the dish
5 tbsp golden syrup

For the crumble topping:
125g plain flour
50g rolled oats
75g cold butter, cubed
50g golden caster sugar
50g soft light brown sugar
25g flaked almonds
25g chopped walnuts
Small pinch of salt

For the crème fraîche:
Zest of ½ orange
1 tbsp golden caster sugar
200ml crème fraîche

Preheat the oven to 200°C/180°C fan. Tip the rhubarb into a buttered oven dish and drizzle over the golden syrup.

In a bowl, rub together the flour, oats and butter with your fingertips until you achieve a crumbly texture – don't overwork it, you want it to stay a bit rough. Stir through both sugars, the flaked almonds, chopped walnuts and pinch of salt.

Spoon the crumble over the rhubarb and spread it out gently. Bake for 40–45 minutes until golden and bubbling at the edges.

While the crumble is in the oven, fold the orange zest and sugar into the crème fraîche; keep chilled until ready to serve.

Treacle Sponge with Stem Ginger & Citrus Zest

SERVES
4

PREP
15
mins

COOK
50
mins

There's something about a treacle sponge that instantly takes you back to school dinners, but it's one of those puddings that has stood the test of time. These days, you'll find it proudly sat on pub menus too, still delivering that same comfort but with a touch more finesse. This version brings in stem ginger for warmth and a hit of citrus zest, and it's finished with plenty of double cream to balance the sweetness. Each ramekin serves 2 people.

175g butter, softened, plus extra for greasing
175g caster sugar
Zest of 1 lemon
Zest of 1 orange
3 eggs
175g self-raising flour
1–2 tbsp milk
75g golden syrup
1½ tbsp stem ginger, finely chopped
Double cream, to serve

Grease 2 large ramekins, about 10cm in diameter and 7cm deep, with butter.

In a large bowl, beat the butter with the sugar, lemon zest and orange zest until pale and fluffy. Add the eggs one at a time, beating well between each addition. Fold in the flour gently, then stir in just enough milk to loosen the mixture slightly – it should drop from a spoon but not be runny.

Spoon half the golden syrup into the base of each ramekin, then scatter over the chopped ginger. Pour the sponge mixture in until just below the rim, leaving room for it to rise. Cover the top of each ramekin with a layer of greaseproof paper and tie securely with string.

Sit the ramekins in a deep pan and pour in enough boiling water to come just over halfway up the sides. Cover with a lid and let them simmer gently for 45–50 minutes, topping up with more boiling water if needed. Remove carefully, leave to settle for a couple of minutes, then turn them out so the syrup runs down over the sponge.

Serve warm with plenty of double cream.

Spotted Dick with Rum-Soaked Currants & Custard

SERVES
6

PREP
30
mins
(+ soaking)

COOK
1¼
hours

This old-school pudding is rich and comforting, steamed so it's soft and fluffy, with rum-soaked currants giving little bursts of flavour. Turning it out of the basin to reveal a golden, steaming sponge is one of those small kitchen moments that never gets old – and when you bring it to the table with warm custard poured over, your family and friends will be very impressed.

110g currants
2 tbsp dark rum
Butter, for greasing
1 tbsp golden syrup (optional)
300g plain flour
10g baking powder
150g shredded suet
75g caster sugar
Zest of 1 lemon
200–220ml whole milk

For the custard:
1 vanilla pod, slit lengthways and seeds scraped out
200ml milk
200ml double cream
6 egg yolks
75g caster sugar
Pinch of salt

● **Cost-saving tip:** *If you can't get vanilla pods, use vanilla extract. 1 vanilla pod is equivalent to 2–3 teaspoons of vanilla extract.*

Put the currants in a small bowl and cover with the rum, leaving them to soak for at least 30 minutes. Grease a 1.2-litre pudding basin with butter, then if you like, drizzle golden syrup into the bottom for extra moisture and sweetness once turned out.

In a mixing bowl, sift together the flour and baking powder, then stir in the suet, sugar, lemon zest and soaked currants. Pour in the milk a little at a time until you have a soft, slightly sticky dough so it stays moist when steamed.

Spoon the mixture into the basin and smooth the top. Cover with a pleated piece of baking paper, tie with string, and top with a damp tea towel, tying again to secure. Place the basin in a large lidded pan and pour in enough boiling water to come two-thirds of the way up the sides. Cover and steam gently for 1 hour 15 minutes, topping up with more boiling water as needed. Keep the simmer gentle rather than boiling hard.

While it steams, make the custard. Add both the vanilla pod and seeds to a pan with the milk and cream, then warm gently until just below simmering. Remove from the heat, leave to infuse for 10 minutes, then strain through a fine sieve to remove the pod and any skin.

Whisk the egg yolks and sugar in a bowl until pale, then slowly pour in the warm infused milk mixture, whisking as you go. Return it all to the pan and cook over a low heat, stirring until the custard thickens enough to coat the back of the spoon. Season lightly with a pinch of salt.

Remove the pudding from the pan, take off the paper, and leave for a minute before turning out. Slice and serve straight away with plenty of the warm custard.

Derbyshire Oatcake & Honeycomb Parfait

SERVES
6

PREP
40
mins
(+ freezing)

COOK
15
mins

Derbyshire oatcakes aren't your average breakfast component. They're big, soft, oaty pancakes that come from the Peak District, somewhere between a crêpe and a crumpet. Derbyshire oatcakes aren't just for breakfast with bacon and cheese (though I'll never say no to that). This one's a sweet twist with honeycomb and hazelnut crumb – creamy, nutty and full of texture.

---

4 Derbyshire oatcakes
50g roasted hazelnuts
200g caster sugar
5 tbsp golden syrup
2 tsp bicarbonate of soda
350ml double cream
350ml whole milk
6 egg yolks
140g caster sugar
1 tsp vanilla extract
Extra honeycomb, to decorate

Preheat the oven to 180°C/160°C fan. Bake the oatcakes on a wire rack for 15–20 minutes on each side until fully crisp. Leave to cool. Cut the chewy centres into 1cm chunks for the parfait and pulse the crisp edges with the hazelnuts to make a coarse crumb.

Line a baking tray with baking paper. Gently heat the sugar and golden syrup in a heavy-based pan over a medium heat without stirring until it turns a deep golden amber, about 5–6 minutes. Take off the heat and quickly whisk in the bicarbonate of soda. Immediately pour the mixture on to the tray and leave it exactly as it is so the bubbles stay. Leave to cool completely until hard, around 30 minutes, then break into chunks.

Line a 1-litre loaf tin with cling film. For the parfait base, heat the cream and milk in a pan until steaming (don't let it come to a simmer). Whisk the egg yolks and sugar in a heatproof bowl over simmering water for 2–3 minutes until pale and airy. Remove from the heat, then slowly pour in the hot cream while whisking continuously. Return the mixture to the pan and cook gently, stirring, until the custard coats the back of the spoon. Stir in the vanilla.

Cool the custard to room temperature, then cover and chill in the fridge until completely cold, at least 2 hours. Whisk the chilled custard for 3–5 minutes until pale, light and mousse-like.

Fold in the 1cm oatcake pieces and most of the honeycomb. Pour into the lined loaf tin, level the top and freeze for at least 6 hours or overnight.

Remove from the freezer 5–10 minutes before serving. Turn out, slice thickly and scatter with the hazelnut oatcake crumb and reserved honeycomb.

Bakewell Tart with Raspberry & Gin Jam

SERVES
10–12

PREP
45
mins

COOK
1
hour

Bakewell's only twenty minutes down the road from me, so it's fair to say I've sampled a fair few of these. My take adds a splash of gin to the raspberry jam for a sharper edge, then keeps the finish classic with flaked almonds and icing sugar.

175g raspberry jam
50ml raspberry gin (2 shots)
160g butter, softened
160g icing sugar, plus extra for dusting
4 eggs (at room temperature)
¾ tsp almond extract
140g ground almonds
40g plain flour
30g flaked almonds

For the pastry:
275g plain flour
55g caster sugar
150g cold butter, cubed
1 egg yolk
2–3 tbsp cold water

First make the pastry. Rub the flour, sugar and butter together with your fingertips until it resembles breadcrumbs. Add the egg yolk and just enough cold water to bring it together into a dough. Shape into a disc, wrap in cling film and chill for 30 minutes.

Roll out the pastry and use it to line a 30cm tart tin that is about 3–4cm deep. Trim the edges neatly, prick the base with a fork and chill again while you preheat the oven to 200°C/180°C fan.

Line the pastry with baking paper and fill with baking beans. Blind bake for 15 minutes, then remove the paper and beans and bake for an additional 10 minutes, or until lightly golden. Cool slightly.

Gently heat the raspberry jam and gin in a small pan. Simmer for 3–5 minutes until slightly thickened and the alcohol has cooked off. It should be spreadable, not runny. Leave to cool, then spread evenly over the pastry base.

Beat the butter and icing sugar together until pale and fluffy. Add the eggs one at a time, beating well after each addition, then stir in the almond extract. Fold through the ground almonds and flour until smooth.

Spoon the frangipane over the jam and level it out. Scatter the flaked almonds over the top and bake for 40–45 minutes until golden and just set in the centre. Leave to cool completely in the tin.

Dust lightly with icing sugar before slicing and serving.

Crumpet & Butter Pudding with Vanilla Ice Cream

SERVES
8

PREP
20
mins

COOK
45–50
mins

Bread and butter pudding has its place, but crumpets do the job even better. They soak up the custard beautifully, turning soft in the middle while the tops crisp up, adding another layer of texture. Scatter in almonds for crunch and raisins for sweetness and serve warm with a scoop of vanilla ice cream.

100g butter, melted and cooled, plus extra for greasing
16 crumpets
80g raisins
50g flaked almonds
6 eggs
220g caster sugar
600ml cream
300ml milk
Zest of 1 orange
2 tsp vanilla extract
Demerara sugar, for sprinkling
Icing sugar, to dust
Vanilla ice cream, to serve

Preheat the oven to 200°C/180°C fan and grease a large baking dish with butter.

Cut the crumpets in half and brush the sides with the melted butter. Arrange them in the dish, slightly overlapping, scattering the raisins and almonds between the layers and making sure the raisins are tucked under the crumpets so they don't burn in the oven.

In a large bowl, whisk the eggs and caster sugar until the mixture is pale. Add the cream, milk, orange zest and vanilla extract and whisk again to combine. Pour this custard over the crumpets, pressing them down gently so they absorb the liquid. Leave to sit for 10 minutes, then sprinkle the top with demerara sugar.

Bake for 45–50 minutes until the custard is just set and the top is golden and slightly crisp. Remove from the oven and dust lightly with icing sugar.

Spoon generous portions on to plates and serve warm, with vanilla ice cream on the side.

Dark Treacle & Honey Tart with Lemon Zest Clotted Cream

SERVES
8–10

PREP
30
mins
(+ chilling)

COOK
45–50
mins

This dessert is very indulgent and I like to use equal parts treacle and honey for a deep richness with a gentle, floral sweetness running through it. A spoonful of lemon-zested clotted cream on the side keeps everything feeling fresh.

275g plain flour, plus extra for dusting
135g cold butter, diced
55g icing sugar
1 egg yolk
2–3 tbsp cold water
300g dark treacle
300g mild runny honey
175g fresh white breadcrumbs
3 eggs, beaten

For the clotted cream:
2½ tbsp icing sugar
Zest of 2 lemons
350ml clotted cream

Rub the flour and butter together with your fingertips until it resembles breadcrumbs, then mix in the icing sugar. Add the egg yolk and just enough cold water to bring it into a dough. Wrap and chill for 30 minutes.

Roll the pastry out on a floured surface to fit a 26–28cm tart tin. Press it into the tin, leaving a little pastry overhanging the edges. Prick the base with a fork and chill again for 20 minutes.

Preheat the oven to 220°C/200°C fan. Line the pastry case with baking paper and fill it with baking beans. Blind bake for 15 minutes, then remove the paper and beans and bake for a further 7 minutes. Trim away the excess pastry. Lower the oven temperature to 200°C/180°C fan.

Warm the treacle and honey gently in a pan until runny, then stir in the breadcrumbs and eggs. Pour the mixture into the pastry case and smooth the top. Bake for 25–30 minutes until just set with a slight wobble in the centre. Leave to cool a little.

For the cream, fold the icing sugar and lemon zest into the clotted cream. Serve generous spoonfuls alongside warm slices of the tart.

Apple & Blackberry Pie with Chopped Walnuts & Elderflower

SERVES
8

PREP
35
mins
(+ 20 mins chilling)

COOK
50–55
mins

Soft, spiced apple and tart blackberry filling meets buttery pastry, crunchy walnuts and a gentle hint of elderflower. A mix of textures and flavours that makes every bite feel a bit special. It's homely, generous and everything a good pub pudding should be.

4–5 medium apples, peeled, cored and sliced (Bramley or cooking apples work well)
250g blackberries
80g chopped walnuts
100g soft light brown sugar
3 tbsp elderflower syrup
2 tsp ground cinnamon
1½ tbsp plain flour
1 egg, beaten, for brushing
2 tbsp demerara sugar, for sprinkling
Cream or custard, to serve

For the pastry:
400g plain flour
200g cold butter, cubed
2½ tbsp caster sugar
1 egg yolk
4–5 tbsp cold water

Preheat the oven to 210°C/190°C fan.

Make the pastry. Rub the flour, butter and caster sugar together in a bowl until the mixture resembles breadcrumbs. Add the egg yolk and just enough cold water to bring it together into a dough. Divide into two pieces, one slightly larger than the other. Wrap and chill for 20 minutes.

Roll out the larger piece of pastry and use it to line a 24–26cm pie dish, letting the edges hang over slightly.

In a large bowl, toss together the sliced apples, blackberries, chopped walnuts, brown sugar, elderflower syrup, cinnamon and flour until evenly coated. Spoon the filling into the pie case.

Roll out the remaining pastry and lay it over the top. Trim the edges and press to seal, then crimp with your fingers or a fork. Cut a few small slits in the centre to let the steam escape. Brush with the beaten egg and sprinkle over the demerara sugar.

Bake for 50–55 minutes until the pastry is golden and the fruit is bubbling up through the gaps. Leave to cool for 15–20 minutes before slicing so the filling settles. Best served warm with cream or custard.

Dark Chocolate Stout Cake with Cream Cheese Frosting

SERVES
10–12

PREP
20
mins

COOK
55–60
mins

I love a good pint of stout – smooth, rich, and satisfying – and this cake captures that same character in dessert form. Dark, indulgent sponge with just the right balance of bitterness and sweetness, finished with a soft, creamy icing that resembles the iconic head of a pint of stout.

250g butter, plus extra for greasing
250ml stout
75g cocoa powder
400g caster sugar
140ml soured cream
2 eggs
1 tbsp vanilla extract
275g plain flour
2½ tsp bicarbonate of soda

For the icing:
1 vanilla pod
300g full-fat cream cheese
125g icing sugar
150ml double cream

Preheat the oven to 180°C/160°C fan and grease and line a 24cm springform cake tin. Pour the stout into a large pan with the butter. Gently melt together, then whisk in the cocoa powder and caster sugar until smooth. Leave to cool slightly.

In a separate bowl, whisk together the soured cream, eggs and vanilla extract until well combined, then slowly pour the mixture into the stout. Sift in the flour and bicarbonate of soda and gently whisk until a smooth batter forms.

Pour the mixture into the tin and bake for 55–60 minutes, or until a skewer comes out with just a few moist crumbs. Cool completely in the tin.

For the icing, slit the vanilla pod in half lengthways and scrape out the seeds. Beat together the cream cheese and icing sugar until smooth, then slowly whisk in the double cream and vanilla seeds until the mixture is thick and spreadable.

Spoon the icing generously over the cooled cake, letting it sit proud on top to resemble the creamy head of a pint of stout.

● **Cost-saving tip:** *If you can't get vanilla pods, use vanilla extract. 1 vanilla pod is equivalent to 2–3 teaspoons of vanilla extract.*

Lemon & Orange Meringue Pie

SERVES
10–12

PREP
40
mins

COOK
35
mins

An absolute classic and one of my favourites. Crisp pastry filled with a citrus curd that's silky, sharp and fragrant, with the lemon's zing softened by a touch of orange. Topped with a mountain of soft meringue, it feels indulgent yet lighter than many other desserts on the menu, which is why it always goes down so well.

For the pastry:
350g plain flour
175g cold butter, diced
70g caster sugar
1 egg yolk
4–5 tbsp cold water

For the filling:
7 egg yolks (keep the whites for the meringue)
325g caster sugar
75g cornflour
450ml water
Zest and juice of 2 lemons
Zest and juice of 1 orange
75g butter

For the meringue:
10 egg whites
550g caster sugar

Rub the flour and butter together with your fingertips until it looks like breadcrumbs, then stir in the sugar. Add the egg yolk and just enough of the cold water to form a dough. Shape into a disc, wrap in cling film and chill for 30 minutes.

Roll the pastry out and use it to line a 28–30cm tart tin. Prick the base with a fork and chill again while you preheat the oven to 200°C/180°C fan. Line the pastry with baking paper and fill with baking beans, then blind bake for 15 minutes. Remove the paper and beans and continue baking for 5–10 minutes more until golden. Leave to cool.

For the filling, whisk the egg yolks in a bowl. In a pan, mix the sugar, cornflour and water, then cook over a medium heat until thick and bubbling. Remove from the heat and whisk in the lemon zest and juice, orange zest and juice, and the butter. Slowly whisk in the yolks, then return the mixture to the pan and cook for 2–3 minutes more, stirring constantly, until it is glossy and thick enough to coat the back of a spoon heavily. Pour into the pastry case and let it cool completely before topping.

For the meringue, whisk the egg whites until soft peaks form, then gradually add the sugar a spoonful at a time until the mixture is thick and glossy. Spoon the meringue on top of the filling, spreading it out to seal the edges, and then swirl the top generously. Bake at 200°C/180°C fan for 20 minutes until golden. Cool before slicing.

Eton Mess with Black Pepper Strawberries

SERVES
4

PREP
30 mins
(+ cooling)

COOK
1 hour

This is one of those desserts that feels effortlessly impressive at a dinner party. You can make it earlier in the day, keep it in the fridge, then bring it out when everyone's ready. It's light, summery and an unmistakably British classic – a real crowd-pleaser, especially with that little twist of black pepper on the strawberries.

---

2 egg whites
110g caster sugar, plus 1 tbsp
450g strawberries
1½ tbsp icing sugar
½ tsp freshly cracked black pepper
2 tsp balsamic vinegar
300ml double cream
1 tsp vanilla extract

Preheat the oven to 140°C/120°C fan and line a baking tray with baking paper. Whisk the egg whites in a clean bowl until soft peaks form, then gradually add the 110g caster sugar, a tablespoon at a time, until the mixture is thick and glossy. It should feel smooth when rubbed between your fingers. Spoon 6–8 meringues on to the lined tray and bake for 1 hour, then turn off the oven and leave them inside to cool completely.

Hull and halve the strawberries, then toss them with the icing sugar, black pepper and balsamic vinegar. Leave for 20 minutes so they soften and release their juices.

Whip the double cream with the tablespoon of caster sugar and the vanilla extract until it just holds soft peaks. Crumble 4 of the cooled meringues into chunks and fold them through the cream.

Spoon into 4 glasses, layering with the strawberries and their juices, then finish with a few extra meringue shards on top.

Buxton Pudding with Custard

SERVES **8–10**

PREP **35 mins** (+ 50 mins chilling)

COOK **40 mins**

A classic from my hometown – shortcrust pastry layered with sharp damson jam and a soft, buttery breadcrumb sponge, baked until golden. Buxton is a historic spa town known for its fresh mineral water and scenic walks through the Peaks, but it's also got a dessert that can hold its own against its more famous neighbour, the Bakewell Tart. This is my take on the traditional version: rich, comforting and perfect for feeding a crowd. Best served warm with a big jug of custard.

For the pastry:
275g plain flour
55g caster sugar
Pinch of salt
150g cold butter, cubed, plus extra for greasing
1 egg yolk mixed with 2 tbsp cold water

For the filling:
233g damson jam
200g butter, softened
200g caster sugar
4 medium eggs
200g white bread (crusts removed), blitzed into fine crumbs

For the custard:
500ml whole milk
1 vanilla pod, slit lengthways and seeds scraped out
6 egg yolks
100g golden caster sugar

- **Cost-saving tip:** *If you can't get vanilla pods, use vanilla extract. 1 vanilla pod is equivalent to 2–3 teaspoons of vanilla extract.*

Start with the pastry. Rub the flour, sugar and a pinch of salt with the cold butter until it resembles breadcrumbs. Add the egg yolk and water and mix just until it comes together, then shape into a disc, wrap in cling film and chill for 30 minutes.

Roll out the chilled pastry and use it to line a greased 23cm tart tin, letting the edges hang over slightly. Chill again for 20 minutes.

Preheat the oven to 190°C/170°C fan. Line the pastry case with baking paper and baking beans and blind bake for 15 minutes, then remove the beans and paper and bake for another 6–8 minutes until pale golden. Trim the edges and reduce the oven to 160°C/140°C fan.

Spread the damson jam evenly over the pastry base. In a bowl, beat the butter and sugar until pale and fluffy, then beat in the eggs one at a time. Fold in the breadcrumbs until fully combined. Spoon the mixture over the jam and smooth the top. Bake for 35–40 minutes until golden and set. Let it rest for 10 minutes before slicing.

To make the custard, heat the milk in a pan with the vanilla pod and seeds until just below boiling. In a separate bowl, whisk the egg yolks and sugar until pale. Slowly pour the hot milk into the egg mixture, whisking constantly. Return it to the pan and cook gently over a low heat, stirring the whole time, until thickened. Do not let it boil. Remove the vanilla pod.

Cut generous slices of the pudding serve with plenty of warm custard.

Earl Grey Crème Brûlée with Shortbread Biscuits

SERVES
6

PREP
25
mins

COOK
1
hour
(+ chilling)

Crème brûlée is one of those timeless puddings that never goes out of fashion. This version is lifted with the floral hit of Earl Grey, with a caramelised sugar top that cracks to reveal silky custard underneath and buttery shortbread biscuits on the side for dipping.

For the crème brûlée:
600ml double cream
200ml whole milk
10 Earl Grey tea bags
1 tsp vanilla extract
6 egg yolks
100g caster sugar, plus extra for topping

For the shortbread:
100g cold butter, cubed
50g caster sugar
150g plain flour
Pinch of salt

Preheat the oven to 170°C/150°C fan. Put the cream and milk in a pan and bring just to the boil. Remove from the heat, add the Earl Grey tea bags and leave to infuse for 10 minutes. When removing the bags, squeeze them gently over the pan to release as much liquid and flavour as possible – don't worry if a few leaves escape into the mix as they'll be strained out later. Stir in the vanilla extract.

Whisk the egg yolks with the sugar in a bowl until pale. Slowly pour in the warm cream mixture, whisking constantly. Strain through a sieve into a jug, then divide between 6 ramekins. Place the ramekins in a deep baking tray and pour in just enough boiling water to come halfway up the sides. Bake for 35–40 minutes until just set with a slight wobble in the middle. Remove, cool, then chill in the fridge for at least 4 hours or overnight.

While the custards chill, make the shortbread. Beat the butter and sugar together until smooth and creamy. Add the flour and salt, then gently work it together until it just forms a dough – don't overmix. Shape into a disc, wrap in cling film and chill in the fridge for at least 30 minutes.

Roll out the chilled dough on a floured surface to about 7–8mm thick and cut into shapes. Place on a lined baking tray, prick each with a fork, and chill again on the tray for at least 30 minutes so they keep their shape. Preheat the oven to 190°C/170°C fan.

Bake for 15–20 minutes until pale golden and crisp. Cool briefly on the tray, then transfer to a wire rack to firm up fully.

When ready to serve, sprinkle each custard with a thin layer of caster sugar. Use a blowtorch or a hot grill to caramelise until crisp. Serve with the shortbread on the side.

Sticky Toffee Pudding with Vanilla Ice Cream

SERVES
6–8

PREP
20
mins

COOK
40
mins

If there's one dessert that sums up the pub for me, it's this. Sticky toffee pudding is right up there with the greats, and it's one of my personal favourites too. Rich, soft sponge with dates running through it, drowned in a glossy toffee sauce, topped with vanilla ice cream and a touch more sauce for good measure – it's the sort of pudding that keeps pulling you back for another spoonful.

175g dates, stones removed
175ml boiling water
75g butter, plus extra for the dish
175g soft light brown sugar
3 medium eggs
250g self-raising flour
1 tsp baking powder
1 tsp bicarbonate of soda
75g golden syrup
125ml whole milk
Vanilla ice cream, to serve

For the sauce:
75g butter
75g soft light brown sugar
2 tbsp golden syrup
1 tsp vanilla extract
150ml double cream

Start by chopping the dates, then place them in a bowl and pour over the boiling water. Leave to sit for 20 minutes, then blend until smooth.

Preheat the oven to 180°C/160°C fan and lightly butter a 1.5-litre baking dish (approximately 30 x 25cm).

In a large mixing bowl, beat together the butter, sugar, eggs, self-raising flour, baking powder, bicarbonate of soda and golden syrup until just combined. Add the blended date mixture and the milk, stirring again until smooth. Pour the mixture into the dish and bake for 35–40 minutes, or until risen and a skewer inserted into the centre comes out clean.

While it bakes, make the sauce. Put the butter, sugar, golden syrup, vanilla and cream into a pan. Heat gently, stirring until the sugar has dissolved and the butter melted. Bring to the boil and let it bubble for a couple of minutes until slightly thickened.

When the pudding is out of the oven, poke holes all over the top with a skewer or fork and pour over about half of the sauce so it soaks in. Serve generous squares of the pudding with the rest of the sauce poured over and a scoop of vanilla ice cream alongside.

Index

Note: page numbers in **bold** refer to illustrations.

D

E

F

G

H

I

J

K

L

M

N

O

P

Q

R

S

T

V

W

Y

Conversion Tables

Weights

METRIC	IMPERIAL
15g	½ oz
25g	1 oz
40g	1½ oz
50g	2 oz
75g	3 oz
100g	4 oz
150g	5 oz
175g	6 oz
200g	7 oz
225g	8 oz
250g	9 oz
275g	10 oz
350g	12 oz
375g	13 oz
400g	14 oz
425g	15 oz
450g	1 lb
550g	1¼ lb
675g	1½ lb
900g	2 lb
1.5kg	3 lb
1.75kg	4 lb
2.25kg	5 lb

Volume

METRIC	IMPERIAL
25ml	1 fl oz
50ml	2 fl oz
85ml	3 fl oz
150ml	5 fl oz (¼ pint)
300ml	10 fl oz (½ pint)
450ml	15 fl oz (¾ pint)
600ml	1 pint
700ml	1¼ pints
900ml	1½ pints
1 litre	1¾ pints
1.2 litres	2 pints
1.25 litres	2¼ pints
1.5 litres	2½ pints
1.6 litres	2¾ pints
1.75 litres	3 pints
1.8 litres	3¼ pints
2 litres	3½ pints
2.1 litres	3¾ pints
2.25 litres	4 pints
2.75 litres	5 pints
3.4 litres	6 pints
3.9 litres	7 pints
5 litres	8 pints (1 gallon)

Measurements

METRIC	IMPERIAL
0.5cm	¼ inch
1cm	½ inch
2.5cm	1 inch
5cm	2 inches
7.5cm	3 inches
10cm	4 inches
15cm	6 inches
18cm	7 inches
20cm	8 inches
23cm	9 inches
25cm	10 inches
30cm	12 inches

Oven temperatures

°C	FAN °C	°F	GAS MARK
140°C	120°C	275°F	Gas Mark 1
150°C	130°C	300°F	Gas Mark 2
160°C	140°C	325°F	Gas Mark 3
180°C	160°C	350°F	Gas Mark 4
190°C	170°C	375°F	Gas Mark 5
200°C	180°C	400°F	Gas Mark 6
220°C	200°C	425°F	Gas Mark 7
230°C	210°C	450°F	Gas Mark 8
240°C	220°C	475°F	Gas Mark 9

Acknowledgements

To my wife Rosie and our daughter Aurora: you're my everything. You keep me grounded, make me laugh and remind me what all this is really for. Thank you for putting up with the messy kitchen, the long hours and the endless talk about food. I love you both more than you will ever know.

To my mum and dad: thank you for the love, endless support, the odd loan, and every kitchen utensil I've 'borrowed' over the years. You've always backed me and I wouldn't be where I am without you. And to my sister and brother, Danielle and Will: thank you for all the love and support you've given me from childhood right through to now. A lot of the dishes and memories in this book started with us growing up together, and it's something I'll always be grateful for.

To my best friend, Jake: your work ethic and the way you push yourself is inspiring and infectious. You're always there for me, a true friend in every sense.

To my in-laws, Jill and Ian: thank you both for everything, your kindness and the encouragement you've always shown me mean a lot. And Ian, thank you for all your words of wisdom over the years – and yes, I do listen to you sometimes.

To my friends and family who've supported me, eaten their way through countless recipe tests, and given honest (sometimes a bit too honest) feedback – thank you. From the early days of many failed attempts to the finished plates you see here, you've been there through it all. Your encouragement, appetite and support have made the book what it is.

To my manager, Harry: thanks for keeping things ticking when I was spinning many plates at once. You've been solid from day one and a big part of making this happen.

To the dream team behind the scenes: Ru, Liv, Anna, Jess, Lucy and everyone at Ebury – you took what started as me filming in my kitchen and turned it into a cookbook I'm genuinely proud of. I couldn't have done it without your guidance and know-how. To Troy, Jess and Thea for the food styling magic, Hannah and Zoe for capturing every shot beautifully, and Louie for finding props that brought the pub and food side of things together perfectly – you've all made this book look even better than I imagined.

And to everyone who's followed along, cooked a recipe, shared a comment or just sent a kind word – you've made this whole thing possible. I dedicate this book to you all. I couldn't have done it without your graft, creativity and belief.

Love George x